JOHN HANCOCK

Friend of Freedom

John Hancock:

ILLUSTRATED BY LOUIS F. CARY

Friend of Freedom

JEANNETTE C. NOLAN

HOUGHTON MIFFLIN COMPANY · BOSTON

NEW YORK · ATLANTA · GENEVA, ILL. · DALLAS · PALO ALTO

Contents

LIBERTY TREE

CHAPTER 1

Summer, 1744

LIBERTY TREE   John Hancock stood at the
window of a small house in Braintree, Massachusetts, and looked out at the village street.*
John was seven, tall for his age and rather thin.
His hair and eyes were brown. In the plainly
furnished room behind him, his nine-year-old
sister, Mary, was setting the table for tea, and
his little brother, Ebenezer, played with some
toys on the floor. Mother was in the kitchen,
boiling water for the teapot and cutting slices
of bread and butter.

Mary glanced anxiously at John. "You're
not frightened, are you, John?" she asked,

* In 1792 the section of Braintree in which John
Hancock was born became part of a new town called
Quincy.

whispering so Mother wouldn't hear. "Boston's only a few miles away, and you won't be with strangers."

"I know," he said softly. "It's all right, Mary. I'll get along all right."

Of course he wasn't frightened! If he felt a bit nervous this afternoon, it was because the world and everything in it had changed so much since the death of his father two short months ago. John's father, the Reverend Mr. John Hancock, had been pastor of the Braintree Congregational Church. The whole village had mourned when he died. But now a new minister had been called to the church. Next week the new minister and his family would move into this small house, which was the Congregational parsonage, and the Reverend Mr. Hancock's sorrowing family would have to move out. Mother had rented a tiny cottage in Braintree for herself, Mary, and Ebenezer. And today John would go to Boston, to live there with his uncle and aunt, Mr. and Mrs. Thomas Hancock.

"It is a sensible plan, John," Mother had

explained. "I am hard pressed for money. Your Uncle Thomas is rich and generous, and your Aunt Lydia is the very soul of kindness. They have no children of their own. They love you and wish to adopt you. They will give you a proper education, as I could not afford to do."

John was surprised and not sure that he liked the plan. He had been born in the parsonage. He couldn't imagine living anywhere else. But he had not said so. He knew that his mother was sad and troubled. He would not add to her many problems.

As the clock in the hall struck three, he saw the horses and the coach rounding the street corner.

"They're coming!" he cried. "They're coming!"

Mother hurried in from the kitchen. "Pick up your toys, Ebenezer," she said, straightening her widow's cap and smoothing her apron. "Mary, pull the chairs to the table. John, bid our guests to step in."

John went to the door and opened it. The

big shiny coach had halted at the parsonage
gate. The coachman leaped down from his
box to help the passengers to alight. Aunt
Lydia got out first. She was a large woman,
dressed in rustling purple silk and a flower-
crowned bonnet. Then Uncle Thomas appeared, stout and red-faced, wearing a curled
white wig and a fine coat with brass buttons.

John bowed to them. "Good day, ma'am.
Good day, sir."

"Dear boy," said Aunt Lydia, leaning to kiss
him on the cheek. "Dear John, such pretty
manners!"

Uncle Thomas was carrying a big parcel tied
with string. "Good day, indeed!" he boomed
in a deep voice. "A wonderful day! I declare,
John, your aunt and I are mighty pleased to
be taking you home with us!"

In the parlor, Mother greeted the guests
warmly, Mary curtsied to them, and Ebenezer
grinned shyly, one finger in his mouth.

"Tea is ready," Mother announced. "Pray
let us be seated."

Uncle Thomas was in gay spirits as they sat

at the table, talking a great deal. "You need have no fears about John," he said to Mother. "We'll take good care of him. He will visit you often, and you and the other children must come to visit us whenever you can."

"Thank you," Mother answered. "My only fear is for John's health. He sometimes has bad headaches. That's why he hasn't yet started to school."

"I can read, though," John said. "Mary taught me to read."

"No," said Mary. "You mostly taught yourself. John is a smart boy, Aunt Lydia."

"Oh, I know he is!" Aunt Lydia said. "And we shall be *so* careful of his health."

When the teapot had been emptied and the bread and butter eaten, Uncle Thomas untied his parcel. Inside were separate paper-wrapped packages, each containing a present. Uncle Thomas had brought something for everybody. For Mother there was a lacy shawl, for Mary a wax doll, for Ebenezer a spinning top and six delicious peppermint sticks. The biggest package was for John. In it were a jacket

and trousers of dark red satin, a ruffled white shirt, white cotton stockings, buckled shoes, and a red straw hat with a white ribbon ornament.

"New clothes, John!" said Mary.

"That's a cockade on the hat," said Aunt Lydia. "A white cockade."

"Try them on, lad," said Uncle Thomas. "See whether they fit you."

John ran into the bedroom, took off his old
clothes, put on the new ones, and returned to
the parlor.

"They fit perfectly!" Aunt Lydia exclaimed.
"Even the shoes!"

"Well, what do you think of them, John?"
asked Uncle Thomas, smiling broadly.

"They're not uncomfortable, sir," John answered. "I suppose I'll get used to them."

Mother was not smiling. She said, "Fine feathers never made fine birds, Brother Thomas."

"Quite true. But I believe that fine birds *deserve* fine feathers," said Uncle Thomas. "I believe that my nephew is a fine bird by nature, and I expect to be proud of him in Boston. And now we had better be on the road or we shall not reach home by dark."

They all walked out to the waiting coach. It was not easy for John to say good-by to Mother and Mary and Ebenezer. He had to swallow a lump in his throat and to pretend not to see the tears in Mother's eyes. Then suddenly he had a bold and interesting thought, and he said, "I want to ride on the box with the coachman."

Mother and Aunt Lydia immediately protested. They said he would tumble off and break his neck. But Uncle Thomas chuckled and clapped him on the shoulder and called him a spunky young fellow.

"Up with you!" said Uncle Thomas. "Hold on tight and you won't tumble."

14

So John got up on the box, the coachman jerked the reins and clucked to the horses, and the coach rolled along the village street. At the corner, John looked back and waved his hand, and saw Mother waving to him from the parsonage gate.

He felt strong and brave. "I'm going to Boston," he told the coachman. "I'll probably have some wonderful adventures."

CHAPTER 2

Exploring

John thought that his Uncle Thomas's house on Beacon Hill was like a castle in a fairy tale. Flowers and blossoming hedges filled the garden. Stone steps mounted to the wide front balcony, and in the marble-floored hall a great staircase wound upward. Velvet curtains hung at the many windows. Each room had a fine fireplace, rugs, and furniture and was lighted at night by dozens of candles in brass holders.

John explored the house from attic to cellar. He made friends with the servants, the cook, the maids, and the butler, whose name was Cato. He explored the stables also, and the barn and cowshed. Seth, the coachman, let him feed the sleek horses, the glossy brown

17

cow, and her timid calf. Seth had a spotted
dog that could do comical tricks, and in the
haymow was a ginger-colored cat with a litter
of cunning kittens.

John was happy, but he did wish that he had
some playmates.

"In Braintree, the boys have games on the
village green," he told Seth. "They wrestle
and run races. It's fun. Aren't there any boys
in Boston?"

"Yes, plenty of them," Seth said. "You'll
soon meet some Boston boys."

One morning at breakfast, Uncle Thomas
said, "John, you and I are going sight-seeing
today. Boston is your town now; you must get
acquainted with it. Seth will drive us in the
coach."

This time John rode inside with Uncle
Thomas. The glass windows of the coach had
been lowered and he had a good view of everything as they swung down from Beacon Hill
and clattered through the cobbled streets.
John was wearing his hat with the cockade and
another new suit, red and white striped. He

was so used to new clothes now that he hardly thought of them at all.

As the horses trotted briskly, Uncle Thomas talked about Boston.

"It is built on a peninsula extending out into Massachusetts Bay and is almost entirely surrounded by water," he said. "The location of any town is important. Because of its location and its deep harbor, Boston has become the principal town in Massachusetts Colony and one of the most famous towns in all the thirteen British colonies in America."

"We're Americans, aren't we, sir?" John asked.

"Yes, we are the American subjects of King George II of England," Uncle Thomas answered. "Each colony has a legislature. The members of the legislatures are elected by the colonists from among themselves, and they make many of our laws. But George II is our king. He chooses the royal governors of the colonies, and the English Parliament in London also has the power to make laws for us."

The Boston streets were crowded and noisy.

John saw carpenters with their ladders and tool kits, porters trundling wheelbarrows, fishermen, sailors, tinkers, merchants, peddlers, ladies whirling by in carriages to the shops and markets. Dogs barked, oxcarts rumbled, the drivers of farm wagons cracked their whips and shouted to their teams.

"Is something exciting going on today?" John asked.

Uncle Thomas smiled and said, "Fifteen thousand people live in Boston. Something exciting is always going on."

As they neared the harbor, Uncle Thomas pointed to the islands that lay offshore: Castle Island, where a regiment of the King's soldiers had their quarters, and Bird Island, which was a nesting place for the seagulls that circled and screamed constantly over the water. He pointed to the warehouses, the shipyards, and the piers and wharves at which vessels of all sorts were moored.

"That's Long Wharf," he said. "Two thousand feet long it is! Large ships can dock there, even when the tide's out. Do you see those big sloops? They're mine. They sail to the West Indies and South America — yes, and to Europe. You may not have known that I'm in the shipping trade? It's one branch of my business. And here's one of my warehouses, on the next pier."

The coach stopped before Uncle Thomas's warehouse and he got out. "I must speak to my clerks," he said. "You may stretch your legs a bit, John. But don't wander far or get into mischief."

John was glad to stretch his legs. It was a lovely morning. The sun shone, and a fresh breeze blew in from the bay. The air smelled of salt water, oil, tar and molasses, and drying fish. John strolled down the pier. He sat down on a coil of rope and watched the seagulls dip and soar.

Four boys of about his size came out on the pier. They stopped and stared at him. Their shirts were dirty, they were barefooted, and their faces were streaked with soot.

One boy laughed and said, "Your hat is silly. You look like a monkey."

John jumped up, surprised and angry. "I do *not* look like a monkey!"

"A monkey," the boy repeated. "Want to fight? I dare you!"

John really didn't want to fight, but he didn't want the boy to think he was a coward. He snatched off his hat, threw it down, and said. "Yes, let's fight!"

The boy doubled his fist and hit John on

22

the nose. John gasped, gritted his teeth, and grabbed the boy in a firm wrestling hold. They swayed and fell in a heap, arms locked. They kicked, grunted, then struggled apart.

"I beat!" the boy yelled, getting up. "I beat!"

"You did *not*. I beat!"

"I can run faster than you!"

John's nose was bleeding a little, but he wiped it on his sleeve and said, "I can run faster than *all* of you. Come on, let's race!"

They all dashed madly to the end of the pier,

23

dodged between casks and barrels, dashed back to the coil of rope, and sank down, breathless. The boy who had fought with John picked up the hat and put it on his own head.

"How do I look?" he asked.

"Like a monkey," John said, grinning. "Do you want that hat? You may have it."

"You mean to *keep?*" said the boy.

"Yes. You did run pretty fast. The hat can be the prize for the race."

"But you ran faster!"

"Keep it," said John.

"Well, gee! Well, thanks!" the boy exclaimed. "You're a good fighter, too."

After that, they sat and talked and watched the seagulls until John thought of Uncle Thomas and said that he must go.

"Come again some other day," the boys said. "We're usually around here."

Uncle Thomas was waiting in the coach. "Where on earth have you been?" he asked. "What have you been doing? You've torn your jacket and where's your hat?"

John explained about the hat.

"You gave it to a little *wharf rat?*"

"Oh, he's not a wharf rat. He's nice," John said. "They're all nice, all my friends now. We had fun."

Uncle Thomas seemed puzzled. He rubbed his chin and said, "Fun? Well, well!"

CHAPTER 3

Boston Seasons

LIBERTY TREE There were boys in the Beacon Hill neighborhood of Boston as well as in the harbor district, and soon John knew many of them.

"My nephew collects friends wherever he goes," Mr. Thomas Hancock once said. "It seems to be a *habit*!"

Mr. Hancock was a dignified person. He liked peace and quiet. Perhaps he was sometimes disturbed by the young visitors who romped over the lawn of his fine house and through the garden. But he didn't complain. Instead, he bought John a small, strong Shetland pony, and told the boys to play mostly in the stable yard, where they could have turns riding the pony.

As for Aunt Lydia, she was certain that John could do no wrong. She never scolded or found fault with him.

"You pamper the child, Mrs. Hancock," said a lady who came to drink tea. "You grant his every wish. You will spoil him."

"Spoil John? Nonsense!" said Aunt Lydia.

"You buy him too many things," the lady insisted.

Aunt Lydia smiled. "He either gives away or shares the things we buy for him. John is quite unselfish."

But John had one wish that Uncle Thomas and Aunt Lydia would not grant. They would not allow him to go to school.

"I promised your mother to be careful of your health," Aunt Lydia reminded him, "and you still have those headaches."

"Not often, ma'am," he said.

"Well, we shall see what the doctor thinks," said Aunt Lydia.

The doctor examined John's eyes, ears, and throat, listened to his lungs, poked him in the ribs, and said, "Mrs. Hancock, the boy is not ill, but he is a bit delicate. I think he had better not start to school for another year."

"He can have lessons at home," said Uncle Thomas. "I'll hire a tutor for him."

Uncle Thomas enjoyed making plans for John's future.

"When you're old enough, I'll send you to Harvard College in Cambridge," he said. "Your father was a graduate of Harvard."

"And are you, sir?" John asked.

"No, I didn't have a college education," Uncle Thomas answered. "My father, like yours, was a Congregational minister and not at all rich. I was a younger son in the family — and really not much of a scholar. So, after I finished at grammar school, I was apprenticed to a printer. That was my first job."

"Were you sorry not to go to college, sir?"

"No, no," said Uncle Thomas. "Business interested me more. I've been very successful in business. But I want you to have both the education and the business success."

John spent the Christmas holidays in Braintree with his mother, Mary, and Ebenezer.

The weather was very cold, with heavy snow. He had a delightful time coasting down the steep hills and skating on the frozen pond. In January he went back to Boston and began lessons with Mr. Edwards, the tutor whom Uncle Thomas had hired.

Mr. Edwards was a pale, slender man of twenty-five. He wore enormous steel-rimmed spectacles, and John secretly nicknamed him "Mr. Owl." Aunt Lydia said she wondered whether Mr. Edwards got proper food at his boardinghouse. "The poor young man looks half-starved!" she said.

Every morning except Saturdays and Sundays, John studied with Mr. Edwards, reading aloud from a primer or writing spelling words and arithmetic sums on a slate. When a month had passed, Mr. Edwards reported to Mr. and Mrs. Hancock that John was obedient and well behaved, but a bit lazy.

"Lazy?" echoed Aunt Lydia. "Oh, no! John hasn't a lazy bone in his body."

"He doesn't work as hard as he should at his books," said Mr. Edwards.

"Oh, dear! Do be patient with him," Aunt Lydia begged.

"I am patient, madam. I will be."

"I shall speak to John," said Uncle Thomas.

Aunt Lydia clasped her hands in alarm. "You won't *punish* him, Thomas? If you must speak, do it *gently!*"

That night, Uncle Thomas very gently told John that he would have to study harder. "Yes, sir. I will," John said. And in the next month he made more progress in his lessons. Mr. Edwards was pleased. He said that, as a reward, he would take John for walks around Boston in the afternoons.

"Good!" Aunt Lydia exclaimed to Uncle Thomas. "And I shall invite Mr. Edwards to eat his noonday meals with us. Maybe we can fatten him up!"

John and Mr. Edwards often walked across Boston Common. The Common was a large open space, almost like a meadow, in the center of the town. The first settlers of Boston had grazed their cattle and sheep there. Now some of it had been fenced off as burial grounds. In other parts public meetings were held. Several churches fronted on the Common. At any hour of the day, bells were to be heard chiming from the church steeples.

The Common was also a training place for the Boston militia.

"The militiamen are the troops of the British colonies," Mr. Edwards said. "They are colonial soldiers, trained by British officers. They drill, march, and parade. In case of need, they protect our citizens."

32

As spring came, on that year of 1745, the number of militiamen on the Common grew.

"They're preparing to march to Canada," Mr. Edwards told John. "In Europe, France and England are at war. The two nations have been enemies and rivals for hundreds of years. Now they're quarreling about their lands in America. Both nations are greedy. France has colonies in Canada on the St. Lawrence River. Lately the French have been raiding the farms of English colonists in Maine, and the Indians have helped them. King George has ordered the colonial militia to stop the raids."

33

"Why do the Indians help the French?" John asked.

"Some of the northern tribes feel that the English colonists have cheated and robbed them," said Mr. Edwards, "and they hate us for it."

In May the Boston militiamen marched to Canada with troops from other New England colonies. In midsummer they returned, flushed with victory. They had captured the great French fort of Louisburg on Cape Breton Island. The people of Boston celebrated the event by ringing the church bells and lighting bonfires on the Common.

"It is the first time in history that a colonial army has ever won a big battle without aid from the King's troops," they said. "It proves that Americans are good soldiers."

One day in August, Mr. Edwards broke the rims of his spectacles. Where could he get them mended?

"At Mr. Paul Revere's shop on Clark's Wharf," said Mr. Hancock. "Revere is a goldsmith. He's a silversmith too. He makes gold and silver plates, spoons, cups, and jewelry. He works with metals of all kinds and he can mend *anything!*"

John went with Mr. Edwards to the Revere shop. And what an interesting place it was! A charcoal-burning furnace stood in one corner of the room. Heating in the furnace were crucibles, or melting pots, in which bars and scraps of metal simmered and bubbled as they melted down into liquids. There were pitchers for pouring the hot metal, and molds and wooden blocks for shaping it as it cooled. There were anvils and bellows, wooden hammers and trimming shears.

Mr. Revere was just lifting a sheet of silver from a flat tray. He motioned to Mr. Edwards and John to be seated on a bench. His son Paul was putting charcoal into the furnace. Paul was a sturdy boy of ten, dressed in a dark shirt, leather breeches, and hobnailed boots. He had red cheeks, black hair, and bright black eyes.

"Any more chores, father?" he said.

"Not now, Paul," said Mr. Revere.

Paul glanced at John. "I'm going out on the wharf to see the dancing bear. Would you like to see it?"

"A real bear? Oh, yes!" John got up eagerly. But Mr. Edwards said, "Better not, John. It might be dangerous."

Mr. Revere was hammering and trimming the sheet of silver to make a cup. He paused. "Why not let him go, sir? The lad will be safe with Paul. The bear is tame, a pet of the sailors from one of the foreign ships anchored in the harbor."

"Very well, then," said Mr. Edwards. "You may go, John."

A crowd had gathered on the wharf, but Paul pushed through and John followed him. Inside a circle of laughing people, the bear was shuffling about on its hind feet, flapping its forepaws, while a blue-coated sailor whistled tunes on a fife. The bear's fur was matted and soiled. A chain dangled from its iron collar. John watched curiously, but he pitied the bear and was glad when the dance ended and the sailor led the unhappy-looking animal away.

"Wild animals should be left in the wilderness, John," said Paul Revere as the boys walked slowly back to the shop.

John nodded. It was exactly what he himself had been thinking. "That bear is probably smarter than most of the people who were laughing at him," he said.

"I go to the North Writing School," Paul said. "Where do you go?"

"Not anywhere — yet," John answered. "But I will next year. At least I hope so!"

Paul said that he had a job, too. He was a bell ringer at Christ Church. "There are six of us chaps to pull the ropes and set those old clappers to banging."

John smiled. "Is it fun?"

"It's work! But I get paid for it, threepence a week. And I work for my father after school and on Saturdays. Not for pay. I'm learning to be a silversmith so that some day I can be my father's partner."

Mr. Edwards was at the shop door, his spectacles mended and on his nose. Mr. Edwards shook hands with Mr. Revere, and John shook hands with Paul. John admired Paul. He knew that now, whenever he heard the bells of Christ Church ring, he would think of Paul Revere who pulled the ropes.

CHAPTER 4

School Days

Shortly before his ninth birthday, John entered the Boston Public Latin School.* Aunt Lydia still fretted about his health, but Uncle Thomas said, "Let him try it. If school seems to harm him, he can study with a tutor again."

John had felt that to study at home with a tutor was a lonely way of getting an education. It had made him seem different from other boys of his age. He wanted to do what everybody else did.

"And I'm sure I can, sir!" he said to Uncle Thomas.

The sixty-five boys of the Latin School were

* Also called the South Grammar School.

41

divided into classes. The day began for them at seven in the morning and lasted until five in the evening, with a brief recess at noon. They had a week's vacation at Thanksgiving and at Christmas, and three weeks off in August. Since John could read and spell rather well, he was put into one of the middle classes, where he studied mathematics, Greek and Roman history, and Latin grammar.

The master, Mr. John Lovell, was very strict. He had a birch rod on his desk. If a boy could not recite his lessons, or if he pouted or whined, Mr. Lovell rapped him on the knuckles, or switched him harshly.

"My school is not a place for rude and idle boys," said Mr. Lovell. "Parents pay me a high fee to teach their sons to be young gentlemen. And that is what I will do!"

The pupils were made to learn their lessons by reading them aloud, over and over. When a whole class studied in this manner, the noise was like the buzzing of a hive of bees. Armed with his birch rod, the master paced up and down the aisles, listening to the voices. If any boy fell silent for a moment, *whack-whack* went the birch rod on his legs and shoulders.

Mr. Lovell's pupils were not fond of him. They said he heard by magic, not with his ears as ordinary human beings do. And he seemed to have an extra pair of eyes in the back of his head. "Maybe he's *not* a human being," the pupils said, grinning. "Maybe he's some sort of *monster!*"

The schoolrooms were poorly lighted at all times, and in winter they were cold. "If the weather is *very* cold, I have a fire," said Mr. Lovell, "but only a small fire. Children should not be too comfortable. It's bad for them."

At four o'clock on school day afternoons, John and his classmates got out their copy-books and inkhorns. They sharpened quill pens and practiced penmanship for an hour. John looked forward to this period. He knew that soon school would be dismissed, and he could go back to the pleasant warmth of Beacon Hill. He was copying Bible verses into his book. His writing had been scraggly and uneven at first, but he had taken great pains with it. Now he wrote a large, clear hand, and his signature was quite beautiful.

John was also learning something about business in these years. Uncle Thomas was his teacher. Mr. Hancock was a very rich and busy man. He bought and sold New England farmland. He owned forests in Maine from which lumber was cut and marketed. He printed and sold books at his Boston print shop, which was called the Bible and the Three Crowns. His ships carried coal, codfish, whalebone, and whale oil to English merchants and to ports in Canada, Holland, and Spain. Returning, the ships brought him cargoes of cloth, tea, paper, sugar, and rum to be sold in the towns of Massachusetts Colony.

Often on Saturdays, John went to his uncle's big general store in Boston. It was always full of shoppers. Boston people said that anything and everything in the world could be found on the counters and shelves of Hancock's store, or in the stockrooms. There were spices, dried fruit, rock salt, flour and lime, dress goods, ribbons and fans, dishes and glassware, guns,

44

swords, nails, rope and wire, fishnets, and a thousand other things.

John loved to wander around, mingling with the shoppers. The clerks were kind to him. He ran errands and tied up bundles. They said he was their assistant. At the rear of the store was an office, where the book-keepers sat on tall stools at their slant-topped desks and made out sales slips and bills.

At noon on Saturdays, John and Uncle Thomas went to a coffeehouse for dinner. Ladies never went to coffeehouses; the diners were all men. John felt old and serious, seated at the table with the men as they ate, drank, talked, and smoked long-stemmed clay pipes.

Sometimes on the way to the coffeehouse, John saw the boys who had laughed at his hat that day on the waterfront. He was delighted that the boys hailed him with hearty shouts. He thought of them as his friends, and he never forgot a friend.

Uncle Thomas said that he was going to buy Clark's Wharf. "I need more docking space for my ships."

"What about Mr. Revere's shop?" John asked.

"I'll not disturb any of the shops and stores on the wharf," said Uncle Thomas.

Once John saw Paul Revere diving from the wharf. Paul was with several big boys. "Come and have a dip, John!" he cried.

"I haven't learned to swim," John said.

"Oh, you must learn," said Paul. "And are you in school now? How do you like it?"

"I don't exactly mind it," said John, "but I like business better."

John spent four years in the Boston Latin School. Then he passed the examinations that would admit him to Harvard College. He had not been the brightest of Mr. Lovell's pupils, but his grades were usually above the average. And he was awarded a leather-bound New Testament for having such neat copybooks. "Excellent writing!" Mr. Lovell had declared.

The Latin School pupils who planned to go on to Harvard were told to report to the college in Cambridge on Commencement Day in July. This was the day when the college

seniors had their graduating exercises. The Harvard Commencement was always as exciting as a circus or a country picnic.

John went to Cambridge with Uncle Thomas and Aunt Lydia. He wore a lavender silk coat and waistcoat, purple breeches, and checkered silk stockings. The Hancocks were driven by Seth in Aunt Lydia's new carriage which Uncle Thomas had ordered for her from London.

"I want a *chariot*," Uncle Thomas had told the English manufacturers. "It must be a

large chariot, for Mrs. Hancock is a large woman. It must be very stylish, with scarlet linings, fringed cushions, and the finest harness. Send me four dozen silver bells to attach to the harness in winter."

Today the bells were not attached, but the chariot was so grand that everyone stared at it. Aunt Lydia did indeed look very large. Her hoop skirts were wide. Her hair was combed in puffs and whirls so high that she could hardly get through the chariot door.

"Really, John, your aunt should have a

carriage just for herself!" muttered Uncle Thomas as they squeezed in beside her.

Travelers from Boston to Cambridge had to ferry across the Charles River at Charlestown. The ferryboats were crowded, and hundreds of people were tramping along the dusty roads. In Cambridge, tents had been pitched on the riverbank. Souvenirs were being sold, acrobats and jugglers were giving exhibitions, and bands of roving musicians played fiddles and horns and begged for pennies.

Aunt Lydia's cook had packed a basket of delicious lunch, which the Hancocks ate in a shady corner of the college grounds. Then, while Aunt Lydia napped in her wonderful chariot, John and Uncle Thomas went to the office of Mr. Holyoke, the president of Harvard, and John signed his name in the register of students for the next term.

John saw other boys of thirteen and fourteen strolling through the halls and looking wide-eyed at everything. He smiled and thought, "This is all new and strange to them, as it is to me. In the autumn, these fellows will be freshmen like me, and for four years we'll be comrades here."

CHAPTER 5

College Student

LIBERTY TREE Ninety boys and young men
were students at Harvard when John Hancock went there. They lived in three brick
buildings that framed three sides of a court
known as Harvard Yard. The college officials
gave the biggest and best rooms to those
students whose parents were either wealthy
or famous, or both. Because Mr. Thomas
Hancock was such a rich man, John had a
very nice bedroom and also a sitting room.
He had a special seat in the chapel and a chair
at the head table in the college dining room,
which was called the Commons. And he was
told that he could march in the front lines of
all college processions.

"I don't think it's fair," John said to a

junior who had smaller quarters near his.

"No, it isn't fair," said the junior.

"It's judging a fellow by what his relatives are, or have done. I think everybody should be on an equal footing."

"The students themselves judge a fellow by how long he's been in the college," the junior said. "The freshmen are greenies. They don't amount to a hill of beans. They're really nothing. They must obey the upper-classmen at all times. You're a freshman, aren't you, Hancock?"

"Yes," John said.

"And I'm a junior; therefore, you must do as I tell you. Here is my wig. Take it to the Cambridge barber and have it curled."

"Now?" John asked. "I was on my way to the library —"

"Now! This minute, Hancock. Run, make haste, or I shall boot you. And when you address me, say 'sir'."

"Yes, sir," John murmured, and off he trotted with the wig.

All that year John and his classmates acted

as servants and messengers for the older students. They were made to feel humble and worthless. They were forbidden to wear hats unless it was raining, snowing, or hailing. They could not play ball in Harvard Yard. They were told that they must never laugh or whistle or sing where any upperclassman might hear them. They must never lift their voices as they went through the halls. And if they received any food from home, they must give most of it to the juniors and seniors.

John grumbled about these rules, but he obeyed them. In fact, he thought them rather amusing. And when he himself became an upperclassman, he gleefully put the "greenies" through their paces.

The Harvard students were a hungry lot. They got up very early in the morning and, without time to eat breakfast, gathered in the chapel for a sermon and prayers. At seven-thirty they had a few moments in which to eat a dry biscuit or two, washed down with coffee, milk, tea, or beer. They spent the rest of the morning in classes. At noon they had a dinner

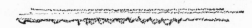

of meat and vegetables in the Commons. At this meal, a huge mug of cider was placed on each of the long tables and everyone drank from it. The mug was scrubbed once a week. The pewter dinner plates were washed only once a month.

In the afternoon, the students had a short recreation period. Then they were shut in their rooms, to study until suppertime. Their supper was a bowl of bread and milk, or a small meat pie and a half-pint of beer.

Aunt Lydia was shocked when she heard about the poor food at Harvard.

"Oh, the dear lads!" she sighed. "All that studying on empty stomachs! And at night, too! Yes, they burn the midnight oil! I wonder they can do it. Well, I shall see that Seth takes a box of cakes and cheese to John every week. Yes, and a roast chicken, and a ham, and some jelly and fruit. Every week — maybe twice a week!"

The arrival of Seth with one of Mrs. Hancock's baskets was loudly cheered by John's friends at Harvard, and many gay "feasts" were given in his rooms. John Adams, a boy from Braintree, was often his guest. John Hancock and John Adams had been friends as children. In years to come they would be drawn together even more closely.

John kept in touch with Braintree and the

members of his family there. His mother had remarried. Her present husband was the Reverend Daniel Perkins. John's sister, Mary, was a young lady now, engaged to be married. His brother, Ebenezer, was a pupil in the village school.

Mr. Thomas Hancock was planning to send Ebenezer to Harvard. "I want my two nephews to be educated at the oldest college in America, and the best," he said.

Mr. Hancock would always demand "the best" of everything for himself and anyone connected with him.

The Harvard professors sometimes lectured to the people of Boston. They spoke to large audiences about the growth of the country. They said the English colonies were changing, becoming larger. More settlers were moving to America from Europe. In Virginia and Pennsylvania, pioneers were pushing westward, claiming western lands. New villages were springing up in places which had been wilderness.

The French had established a chain of trading posts and forts on the Mississippi River and in the Ohio River valley. The English colonists feared the powerful French. It was thought that there soon might be another European war. If France and England fought again, the war might spread to America. In Philadelphia, Benjamin Franklin, a very wise American, was advising the English colonies to unite for their protection.

"We must join — or die," warned Benjamin Franklin.

In 1754 Robert Dinwiddie, the royal governor of Virginia Colony, wished to build a fort at the Forks of the Ohio River. Before he could begin, French soldiers erected a French fort on the exact spot which Dinwiddie had chosen. Aided again by the Indians, the French defeated an army of British and colonial troops in the Ohio Valley. This was the start of a new and bloody rivalry between the two nations. In American history it would be recorded as the French and Indian War.

The outbreak of the war did not interrupt

John's education. His years at Harvard were pleasant and seemed to fly by as if on wings. Soon he was seventeen and about to be graduated.

"My, my!" said Aunt Lydia. "I can't believe it, John."

He laughed and said, "No more can I."

His Commencement Day was sunny and mild. At eleven o'clock in the morning, all the college students walked, two by two,

across the campus to the old meetinghouse for the graduation exercises. The seniors went first. As did his classmates, John wore a black gown, but no hat. His hair was powdered and brushed back in a pigtail, with a black ribbon tied to the pigtail.

As always, crowds of people had come to Harvard from Boston and nearby towns. The royal governor of Massachusetts, Sir William Shirley, with twenty mounted soldiers waited at the church to greet the students. The soldiers' coats were scarlet, with chalk-white sashes. Their swords gleamed in the sunshine. Walking behind the students, like a shepherd tending his flock, was the Harvard president, Mr. Holyoke.

Governor Shirley bowed to Mr. Holyoke. Mr. Holyoke and all the professors and all the seniors bowed low to the governor.

It was hot inside the church and the exercises lasted for four hours. There were prayers and speeches, and songs by the choir. Then the graduates came forward to receive their diplomas. Mr. Holyoke asked each graduate ten questions in Latin, to which the answers had to be in Latin also.

John could see Aunt Lydia and Uncle Thomas in the crowded church. He knew they were thinking about him, hoping he would do well when his name was called. But they need not have worried. As he received the diploma from Mr. Holyoke, John answered all his questions without a single mistake.

"Oh, how proud we are, John!" said Aunt Lydia later. "And how smart of you to reel off so much Latin!"

"Yes, my boy," said Uncle Thomas. "You've never disappointed us and I'm sure you never will."

CHAPTER 6

Young
Mr. Hancock

After John was graduated from college, he went to work in the big Hancock store.

"The usual term of an apprentice is seven years, John," said Uncle Thomas. "You will not be my apprentice, but if you can learn all about my business in seven years, I shall think of you as my junior partner."

"Oh, I can, sir!" John answered.

To himself he said that he would show how fast he could learn the business! He was interested in it, interested in the Hancock ships and their voyages to other lands. He was sure that he would like being a merchant.

"And I'll be successful," he told himself. "I must be, if only for Uncle Thomas's sake. I must repay Uncle Thomas for all he is doing for me."

John's first job was as a bookkeeper in the "compting room." He had a high desk in the row of high desks. For ten hours each day he sat on a high hickory stool and added long columns of figures, or copied orders and bills in his clear, neat writing.

The other bookkeepers teased him good-naturedly.

"Young Mr. Hancock, starting at the bottom of the ladder!" they said, laughing about his ink-stained fingers and the extra pen that he had tucked behind his ear.

"At the very bottom," he said. "But watch me climb!"

Yes, he was "young Mr. Hancock" now, taller than Uncle Thomas — and a great deal thinner! "Slim as a bean pole," so Aunt Lydia described him. "Doesn't eat as he should!" He wore a white wig, just like his Uncle Thomas's. Indeed, he owned half a dozen wigs and had a manservant to see that they were always clean and freshly brushed.

John and Uncle Thomas went to business together every morning. Seth whisked them downtown in the coach, or in the red-wheeled cart that Aunt Lydia had given John on his eighteenth birthday. At evening, Seth reappeared and whisked them back to Beacon Hill.

This "young Mr. Hancock" was said to be the most fashionable youth in Boston. His clothes were the best that could be bought, and colored like the rainbow. Many people thought he was handsome, and his friends were too many to be counted. He danced well, and his manners were polite. He was invited to teas, suppers, and balls. But in company he was rather quiet and seemed to be more at ease with men than with women. He enjoyed outdoor sports such as hunting, fishing, and boating. Sometimes, but not often, he escorted a young lady to a lecture or a concert.

Aunt Lydia said that John was shy about

girls. She said he spent too much of his spare time at home with her and Uncle Thomas.

"You should be thinking of getting married, John," she told him. "Look around for a sweetheart. Fall in love. Or shall I choose a wife for you?"

"Oh, no!" he said. "Heavens, no! When I want a wife, I'll find one for myself!"

During these years, England and France were at war both in Europe and in America. The English king sent troops to America. The colonial militiamen reinforced the English regiments, fighting with them against the French and Indians in the North and the West. Many Americans were killed and more were wounded. And one young officer, Colonel George Washington of Virginia, became known throughout the colonies as a brave and able military commander.

In September, 1759, at Quebec in Canada, the English armies defeated the French. With this battle, the war in America ended, though several years would pass before the European conflict was over.

Somehow, the French and Indian War seemed to unite the American colonies as nothing else had ever done. It made them feel closer to one another. They had come to feel that they weren't entirely dependent upon the English king or the laws made for them by the British Parliament.

But for American shipowners the war had been troublesome. Merchant ships had been in danger as they crossed and recrossed the ocean. Many ships were attacked or seized and their cargoes lost.

"We couldn't get mail back and forth," Mr. Thomas Hancock said to John. "We can't, even yet! I have agents who are transacting business for me in England. At least, they're supposed to transact it, but I hardly ever hear from them. I wish I could *talk* to them."

"Why don't you go to England, sir?" John asked.

"I don't want to. I don't fancy the voyage."

"Let me go for you, Uncle Thomas."

Mr. Hancock frowned. "It would be risky. And what would your Aunt Lydia say?"

"Oh, I could quiet her fears. The ship *Benjamin and Samuel* is due to sail in June, isn't it?"

"Yes. Well," said Mr. Hancock, "I'll get passage for you."

John sailed from Boston on June 2. The *Benjamin and Samuel* was a cargo ship and accepted few passengers. Lying at anchor at Clark's Wharf, the vessel had looked very large, but once it was out on the sea, it seemed tiny, a toy boat at the mercy of waves and wind.

Fortunately the weather was good. John reached London on July 12 and wrote at once to Aunt Lydia, saying that the voyage had been without accident: "And I was only a little seasick."

In London he met Uncle Thomas's agents, and found lodgings in a good hotel. He liked the city and he was never lonely. The agents introduced him to their families and friends, who treated him with consideration and respect. He went to museums, theaters, and the opera and was a guest at house parties.

"And at last," he wrote in a letter to Aunt Lydia, "in the Thames River, I have learned to swim!"

In October, King George II died. The English people had not been very fond of George II, but they mourned for him. Londoners wore bands of black on their hats and coat sleeves. John bought black bands for his own hat and coat sleeve and went to the funeral, where he was seated with officials of the British government. George II's grandson was proclaimed as the new king. He was twenty-two years old and would be crowned as George III.

Writing to Uncle Thomas, John said: "It is thought that the new king will be more popular than his grandfather was. The coronation will probably be in April. I shall stay here for it, as I may never have the chance to see so magnificent a sight again."

But the winter was damp and dreary, and the London fogs were bad for John's headaches. By the time spring came, he was dreaming of home.

When it was announced that the crowning of George III had been postponed until the autumn, he decided to wind up his business affairs and go back to America.

In July, just a year after his arrival in London, John boarded a westbound ship, the *Boscawen*. The voyage was stormy, and it was nearly three months later that the *Boscawen* sailed into Boston Harbor.

Aunt Lydia and Uncle Thomas welcomed him joyfully and exclaimed over the gifts he

had brought them — a beaded scarf and mitts
for Aunt Lydia, and a gold-knobbed cane for
Uncle Thomas. In his trunk were presents for
his mother, and for his sister and brother. And
he had remembered all the Beacon Hill servants. There was a French horn for Cato and
a cap and muffler of Scotch plaid for Seth.

That evening he walked with Aunt Lydia
in the garden. It was October, and most of
the flowers were gone. Aunt Lydia picked a
small bunch of asters and some ferns.

"It is wonderful to be at home," John said.

"You have come none too soon, dear boy,"
said Aunt Lydia. "Do you see how pale your
uncle is? And how he leans on the new gold-
knobbed cane? He is not well, John."

"Oh, I'm sorry!" John said. "I must help
him. I have worked with Uncle Thomas in the
Hancock business for seven years. Maybe now
he will let me take the heaviest loads on my
shoulders."

CHAPTER 7

Boston Merchant

LIBERTY TREE In the summer of 1764, Mr. Thomas Hancock died. John had loved his Uncle Thomas; he grieved for him. Aunt Lydia was so sad that for weeks she did nothing but weep. She clung to John. He was the only person who could comfort her.

The lawyers read Mr. Hancock's will. He had willed the Beacon Hill mansion and its furnishings, his horses and carriages, his silver, and a large amount of money to Aunt Lydia. He had given cash and land to Ebenezer and to other relatives and faithful servants. Funds had been set aside for the church he attended, for Harvard College, and for several charities. Everything else he owned, the Hancock stores, a fleet of thirty ships, wharves and warehouses, farms and forests, he left to his nephew John.

So, at twenty-seven, John Hancock became the richest man in Massachusetts, and one of the richest men in America.

Aunt Lydia begged him to take his uncle's place as master of the Beacon Hill house. "You'll live here?" she asked, through her tears. "You'll manage things for me, won't you?"

He patted her hand. "Of course I will."

He found that he was expected to take his uncle's place in other ways — as a member of the Merchants Club, as a selectman of Boston and director of the town government, as an advisor to the schools and the hospital. He had always had friends among the poor people, and he was even more generous by nature than Uncle Thomas had been. Now he fed and clothed many poor families. He let them cut firewood from his forests. He was particularly thoughtful of orphaned children, widows, and the old and the sick.

"He is our squire," the poor people said. "Young Squire Hancock."

John joined some of the political clubs that were forming in Boston. Americans were feeling restless, not sure about the future. The new King of England, George III, had proved to be harsh and domineering in his treatment of his American colonists. At the end of the French and Indian War, there had been regiments of British troops in the colonies. These soldiers still remained stationed in American towns, and the colonists were taxed to pay for their wages and their upkeep.

King George said the soldiers would protect the colonists from further raiding by the Indians. But the colonists said, "We don't need or want British troops here. Has the King the right to tax us for this purpose? There are more than a million and a half people in the thirteen colonies — and we are not represented in Parliament. We should not be taxed at all by a government in which we have no voice!"

The political clubs met at the Green Dragon Tavern, at the Salutation Tavern, and in the Long Room above the print shop where the Boston *Gazette* was published. One of John's clubs included the lawyer James Otis, Dr. Joseph Warren, John's old friend Paul Revere, and John Adams whom he had known in Braintree and at Harvard. John Adams was now a lawyer, with an office in Boston.

Another member of this club, and its leader, was Samuel Adams, a cousin of John Adams's. Samuel Adams was middle-aged and intelligent. He had a keen mind and a sharp tongue. He hated King George of England. He hated all kings. He felt that the American colonies should be completely independent.

"And we will be!" he said. "Liberty! I don't know when or how we'll get it. I cannot see that far ahead. But I know that it will come!"

In March, 1765, the English Parliament passed the Stamp Act. According to this act all legal papers, books, newspapers, playing cards, and a dozen other items sold in America after November 1, 1765, must be printed on stamped paper. The paper was to be sold by persons whom English officials would appoint. The money paid for it would go to the King. The colonists were told that anyone who did not comply with this act, when it became law, would be arrested and might be tried in the courts without a jury.

Americans were angry about the Stamp Act. The Massachusetts political clubs spoke out against it. An English nobleman, Sir Francis Bernard, was the royal governor of Massachusetts. The lieutenant governor, Thomas Hutchinson, was a native of Boston but a loyal supporter of the King.

Samuel Adams and his circle discussed the Stamp Act in the months before November, 1765.

"It is the worst sort of taxation without representation," John Hancock said one day at the Salutation Tavern.

"It is wrong," said John Adams. "Trial by jury has been guaranteed to British subjects as long as there has been an England."

"And we are British subjects, not slaves,"

said John Hancock. "I will not be a slave! I have a right to the privileges of the English Constitution and, as an Englishman, I will enjoy them!"

Samuel Adams nodded. "Well spoken, Hancock!"

"Yes, yes!" cried Dr. Warren. "Hurrah!"

Paul Revere said there was grumbling and growling in the waterfront district. Boston folk were always easily excited. Sometimes the town had been the scene of riots and had echoed to the shout of *"The mob! The mob is out!"*

"Andrew Oliver has been appointed to sell stamped paper in Boston," Revere said. "Oliver is a friend of Lieutenant Governor Hutchinson's."

"He is also related to Hutchinson," said Samuel Adams. "Oliver married Hutchinson's sister."

Paul Revere went on: "You know that giant elm tree in Essex Street? The people are calling it the Liberty Tree. Twice last week they gathered there. The second time they tramped to Oliver's home and broke his windows. Oh, they were as mad as wet hens!"

"All the colonies resent the Stamp Act, Paul," said John Hancock. "They're all mad as wet hens. In Virginia, Patrick Henry made a stirring speech against it to his fellow members of the legislature. Patrick Henry is a great orator. The Virginia legislators voted not to obey the law and to take the consequences, whatever they may be."

"I don't believe the Stamp Act can be enforced anywhere," Samuel Adams said grimly. "It will have to be repealed. But until that happens, we're likely to have more rioting."

In the summer, the crowds around Boston's Liberty Tree were bigger and noisier. John Hancock heard that Sir Francis Bernard was frightened, had left town, and was hiding in the British fortress on Castle Island. But Lieutenant Governor Hutchinson said, "Braggarts and bullies cannot scare me. The King is our ruler; his laws must be heeded."

One hot August night wild yells resounded in Boston: *"The mob! The mob is out!"* Led by a drunken shoemaker named Mackintosh, a line of jeering, hooting men rushed upon Thomas Hutchinson's house. They were armed with sticks, hatchets, and axes. They pulled down the trellises and arbors in his garden. While Hutchinson, his family, and his servants were escaping through the

kitchen door, the mob pushed into the house and began to wreck it. Chairs, tables, beds, rugs, curtains, and pillows were flung from the windows into the street. Jewelry was stolen, books and portraits were burned. China and glass were smashed. The pantry and cellars were robbed of food and wine.

The house had been as fine as any in Boston. By morning, it was only an ugly skeleton of floors and bare walls, the slate roof pried off and the chimneys toppled into the shrubbery.

Next day the whole town talked of the plundering of Thomas Hutchinson's house.

"It's dreadful, John!" said Aunt Lydia at dinner. "I had Seth drive me there to look at it. Oh, it is a *shame!*"

John agreed. "Yes, it is. I think the Stamp Act is wrong and should be opposed. But I don't like to see anybody's property destroyed."

"I've known Thomas Hutchinson for years," said Aunt Lydia. "He and your Uncle Thomas were boyhood friends. Hutchinson is a stiff, cold man, but he's not really bad. Nor is he to blame for the Stamp Act."

"No, I suppose he's doing what he thinks it is his job to do. Now that Sir Francis Bernard has taken to his heels, Hutchinson is the King's man in Boston. The King issues orders. Hutchinson has to carry out the orders. But you may be sure that he will be blamed for what the King does! The people can't strike at the King, who is 'way off in England. But they can and will strike at his officials in the colonies."

"Oh, what a muddle we're getting into!" Aunt Lydia exclaimed. "I'm sorry that the Hutchinson house was wrecked!"

"So am I," said John. "I wish I somehow could make up to the Lieutenant Governor for his losses yesterday."

In October, a Stamp Act Congress was held in New York. Nine of the colonies sent delegates to the Congress. The delegates drew up documents which declared that the colonists could not be taxed except by their own legislatures.

In November, the Stamp Act went into effect and became a law. But, as Samuel Adams had told his friends at the Salutation, the law couldn't be enforced anywhere. Americans were thinking more and more about liberty. In a hundred towns, people had "liberty trees" or "liberty poles" to show their love of freedom. They sang songs about liberty and wore peaked caps known as "liberty caps." No stamped paper was ever sold, and in March, 1766, Parliament repealed the Stamp Act.

Most Americans felt that with the Stamp Act's repeal their troubles with the King and Parliament were over.

"No," said John Hancock, "we will simply be taxed for something else. The King does not understand us. He has never visited America. Once the colonies were small and weak. The King thinks of them as still small and weak. He seems to think of the colonists as children — and of himself as the father who must look out for us. The fact is, we have grown up and want to look out for ourselves! Sometimes if a father is too stern with his grown-up children for too long — the children will rebel."

CHAPTER 8

Two Ships

John Hancock was not mistaken about King George's intention to tax the colonists. In 1767, Parliament passed the Townshend Acts. One of these measures laid a tax on oil, paper, glass, painter's colors, and tea. Another said that a customs commission would be set up at the port of Boston to collect the taxes and to prevent smuggling. The commissioners would have "tidesmen," who would inspect the cargoes of all ships docking at the wharfs. If the tidesmen discovered smuggled goods, the shipowners would be arrested.

"The people here are hot-tempered," said the commissioners. "They may make a fuss over the Townshend Acts."

"And why not?" John Hancock asked friends of his who were shipowners. "You may do as you like, sirs. But I have told the captains of my ships that I will not have any spying rascal of a tidesman pawing over my cargoes. I will not have it!"

When one of John's ships, the *Lydia,* arrived at the Hancock wharf one April day, two tidesmen boarded her. The *Lydia* was a brigantine, or twin-masted vessel, that sailed in the West Indies. Her captain's name was Scott.

"We've come to inspect your cargo, Captain," the tidesmen said.

"Oh, no you won't!" said Captain Scott. "Mr. Hancock's against it. Inspect this cargo and Mr. Hancock will slice you up like mincemeat and swallow you down."

The tidesmen, Owen Richards and Robert Jackson, said, "We've got our orders."

"And I've got mine!" Captain Scott called to a sailor who was scrubbing the deck. "Mr. Hancock's in yonder warehouse. Go fetch him!"

John was at his desk when the sailor darted into the warehouse.

"Mr. Hancock, sir! Come! The customs men are about to search us!"

"What!" John dropped his pen. "They'll do no such thing!"

He strode instantly to the wharf, where he shouted so furiously and frowned so fiercely that Richards and Jackson took to their heels. As he was returning to the warehouse, he stopped to speak to a fisherman at the edge of the water. This was Jamie Wilkins. As did John Hancock, Wilkins belonged to the Sons of Liberty, a group of Americans who had banded together to resist all laws which they believed to be unjust to the colonists. Starting as a small organization, the Sons of Liberty had rapidly grown. Now there were groups of the sort in several New England towns. Most of the members were good men, though some were rough and crude.

"Hello, Mr. Hancock," said Jamie Wilkins. "Something wrong on your bonny boat?"

"No," John answered. "There might have

been a scrap — if the tidesmen hadn't run."

Mr. Wilkins grinned and wagged his head. "Ah, they're a cowardly lot, sir. But tricky! Best keep an eye peeled for 'em!"

John had a great deal to do that day. He did not get home until nine o'clock. Aunt Lydia had saved supper for him and she had made an apple tart for his dessert. He was never a hearty eater, but apple tart was a dish he liked. As he lifted the first spoonful to his mouth, Cato entered the dining room to say that someone was at the door, asking for Mr. Hancock.

"It's Jamie Wilkins, sir. He said — "

But Mr. Wilkins had followed Cato into the dining room. He looked embarrassed. He bowed to Aunt Lydia. "Excuse me, madam. Excuse me, Mr. Hancock, sir, for disturbing your meal. I thought you'd want to know that as soon as it was dark, Owen Richards sneaked aboard the brigantine. I was on the pier and saw him."

John was surprised. "Did Captain Scott see him?"

"I reckon not, sir. The captain and crew may be sleeping. There's no light on the ship."

John flung down his napkin and rose to his feet. "Get my hat, Cato. Come, Wilkins. And you too, Cato. No, no, Aunt Lydia, I can't wait to eat the tart. But don't worry, everything will be all right."

On the way to the wharf, he chanced to meet eight more Sons of Liberty. "Come with us," John invited, and they went gladly.

They boarded the ship. John awakened the captain and the crew, who were asleep in their berths.

"It was a long voyage, Mr. Hancock," said Captain Scott. "We were all very tired — "

"You should have had a guard posted," John said. "You have been careless. But never mind that now. Richards is down in the hold. Get him up here at once!"

Six sailors hastened down into the vessel's hold. There were sounds of bumps and scuffling. Then Richards was hauled on deck.

"Well, tidesman," John said, "so you want

to inspect my brigantine? I have decided to let you do it — and these friends of mine will help you."

Richards stared at Mr. Hancock's friends, who were scowling, their fists doubled. Richards had heard stories about the Sons of Liberty. They threw stones and broke windows. If they got really angry, they broke bones! Some of them had marched in Mackintosh's mob. One customs collector had been tarred and feathered by them.

Richards moved to the rail of the deck and jumped over the rail. He landed on the wharf. Though it was now eleven o'clock, the wharf was crowded with people. Richards had a hard time getting through the crowd. His toes were tramped on, his eye was blacked, the sleeves were ripped from his coat. He reached the street and dashed for his home, thinking that he was lucky to escape with his skin in one piece!

Laughing and singing, John's friends walked back to Beacon Hill with him and wished him good night.

"I thank you, boys," he said, "but entreat you not to wake the town. Sweet dreams!"

John Hancock had defied the customs commissioners, but they firmly believed that he was smuggling. "We haven't finished with him," they said. "We will watch him."

In May one of his sloops, the *Liberty*, docked at the wharf. This time a tidesman named Kirk was sent to inspect the cargo. Captain Marshall of the *Liberty* grabbed Kirk the minute he stepped on deck, and pushed him into the cabin and nailed up the cabin door. When the cargo was all unloaded, Captain Marshall opened the cabin door.

"Tell the commissioners that we brought twenty-five casks of wine from Madeira, and Mr. Hancock will pay the tax on it," said Captain Marshall.

"I think you brought more than twenty-five casks," Kirk objected. "You could have unloaded that many casks in two hours, but you were a half day at it. I heard the hoist creaking. My guess is that you brought a hundred casks — "

"Tidesman," said Captain Marshall, "what you think or guess is of no interest. If you're not an idiot, you'll keep your mouth shut."

For a month, Kirk said nothing. Then he told the commissioners that he hadn't inspected the *Liberty's* cargo because he had been imprisoned in her cabin. "But I think Captain Marshall's statement about the casks is a lie," he said. The *Romney,* a fifty-gun British warship, was anchored in Boston Harbor. On orders from the commissioners, sailors from the *Romney* cut the *Liberty* from her moorings and chained her fast at the *Romney's* side.

Again John Hancock's friends, and even more of them, were out. They showered the British sailors with rocks, bricks, and mud. "Leave Hancock's sloop alone!" they shouted. "She's at her own wharf. You have no right to capture her!"

They turned upon the commissioners, shouting, "Is this war? Are we at war?"

A little boat with an orange sail lay at the dock. It belonged to one of the customs men. The angry crowd hauled it out of the water and through the streets to John Hancock's house and burned it in front of his door. The noise was so frightening that the commissioners, with their families, hurried to Castle Island and hid in the fortress where Governor Bernard was hiding.

Shortly afterward, the attorney general of Massachusetts had John Hancock arrested.

"I charge you with smuggling, and with insulting the King," said the attorney general. "You will be tried in the admiralty court. If you are guilty, you will have to pay an enormous fine."

"I am not guilty," John said. "I have not violated any law. I have not insulted King George, but the King's officials have robbed me of a ship."

He was tried in 1769. John Adams was his lawyer. The trial lagged on for months, and stories about it were published in many American and English newspapers. Kirk, the tidesman, was the chief witness. He was still quite nervous and could not swear to the

Liberty's cargo, for he hadn't seen it at all, and guesses were not much good in a court of law. No one else seemed to know anything about the incident, but John Hancock insisted that he had done nothing wrong, and most of the colonists felt that he was telling the truth.

"John Hancock is not being tried for smuggling," they said. "He is being tried because he is a patriot."

At last the court dismissed the case.

The *Liberty* was never restored to John Hancock. She vanished from Boston Harbor. No one knew where she had gone. Months later, a ship of the same size and style, but flying the British flag, sailed into the harbor and then sailed away.

"The sloop is British," said the customs commissioners. "Her name is the *Gaspee*. Providence, Rhode Island, is her home port."

But the fishermen and workers around the Boston docks said, "British nonsense! It's the *Liberty* repainted. It's John Hancock's ship that they stole from him!"

CHAPTER 9

Shots in the Night

LIBERTY TREE At about the time of John Hancock's arrest, two regiments of British soldiers were transferred from Canada to Boston. They came in seven British battleships. The whole town was out to see them as they paraded up the Long Wharf, drums beating and fifes squealing.

Aunt Lydia sat in her grand chariot, driven by Seth, with her nephew beside her. "But why are the soldiers here, John?" she asked, gazing at the bright red uniforms.

John smiled. "I suppose it's because King George thinks that the Bostonians are the very naughtiest of all his naughty colonists."

"Well, we do seem to be always ready to boil over," Aunt Lydia said. "Will things quiet down now?"

"I'm afraid not," John answered. "Not while we are taxed unjustly. The King expects us to obey the laws that Parliament makes for us, but we want to make our own laws."

Aunt Lydia sighed. "Do all the people in England hate us?"

"No, no! Many of them are very friendly to the colonies. They wish that the King and Parliament would be kinder to us."

"And there are people in America, like Lieutenant Governor Thomas Hutchinson, who feel that George III is their king by the grace of God and that he can do no wrong. Isn't it odd?" Aunt Lydia's eyes were on the marching redcoats. "I wonder if they will be happy in Boston," she said.

The British soldiers were not happy at all in Boston. They had no barracks in which to live. Their officers had said that they would be housed in private homes, but the Bostonians refused to take them in. Soon it was winter and they had to camp wherever space could be found, in tents on Boston Common, in attics, cellars, stables, vacant warehouses, in the halls and on the steps of the Town House.

They were tormented by the Sons of Liberty, teased by Mackintosh's rowdies. "Lobsters," they were called: "Hi, you *lobsters!*" Angry and chilled, and without enough to do, the soldiers gambled and drank, and quarreled among themselves and with anyone who crossed their path.

March 5, 1770, was a day of very cold weather. Snow fell in the morning, but at evening the sky cleared. At night the moon shone. John Goldfinch, a young English captain, walked in the moonlight from his post in Brattle Square to have a word with the guards in King Street.

Captain Goldfinch was a good military officer, but it was said of him that he didn't always pay his debts. Now, as he rounded the corner, a ragged boy jumped at him and grabbed him by the sleeve.

"You owe my master money!" said the boy shrilly. "Why don't you pay him?"

Captain Goldfinch recognized the boy. He was an apprentice in the shop of Monsieur Piemont, a French barber. It was true that Captain Goldfinch owed money to Monsieur Piemont, but he shook himself loose from the boy's grasp and said, "Begone!"

The boy began to scream: "Robber! Thief!"

Captain Goldfinch walked on, but a sentry named Hugh Montgomery had heard the outcry. Montgomery ran from his sentry box near the Town House. He caught the boy and slapped his face.

The boy sank to the ground and howled, "Murder! *Murder!*"

Instantly people came streaming into King Street from all directions, shouting that a British sentry had murdered a Boston child. They would not listen to Captain Goldfinch's explanations. The barber's apprentice got up and slipped away, but the crowd pushed about in the square in front of the Town House, repeating "Murder! *Murder!*"

Then the bell in the steeple of Old South

Meeting House began to ring. More people scrambled out of their houses, some with buckets of water, believing that the town was on fire. A gang of sailors appeared, yelling at the top of their lungs. They surrounded Montgomery, who was pale with terror and rage.

The day had been a hard one for Montgomery. Snowballs, oyster shells, and chunks of ice had been thrown at him by the rowdies. Now he was hungry and cold, and facing the mob alone.

"Come any nearer and I'll blow your brains out!" he cried.

The sailors roared with laughter. "Shoot, lobster! Shoot if you dare!"

A huge man named Crispus Attucks advanced toward Montgomery with a stick. He poked the stick into Montgomery's ribs and said, "I'll have one of your claws, lobster!"

There was more laughter, and several voices shouted, "Kill him! Kill the lobster!"

Montgomery shrieked, "Main guard! *Main guard, turn out!*"

Captain Preston, officer of the day, came racing into King Street with the seven soldiers who were the main guard. Crispus Attucks struck at Preston, but missed him and knocked down Montgomery. Attucks and Montgomery wrestled and struggled in the snow. Then Montgomery got up, his gun in his hands — and somewhere a voice cried, *"Fire!"*

Montgomery fired two bullets through Crispus Attucks' chest. Attucks dropped, dead as a stone.

106

There were more shots, other dropping
figures. The snow was patched with blood-
stains. Alarm drums thumped. Soldiers with
rattling guns seemed to be everywhere. Somebody ran to get Thomas Hutchinson. In a
little while the lieutenant governor was seen
making his way to the Town House and up the
stairs to the balcony.

"Citizens of Boston —"

107

Suddenly the crowd was silent, looking up at Hutchinson.

"Go to your homes!" he said gravely. "Let the law settle this thing. Blood has been shed and awful work done this night. Go home! Tomorrow the law will take its course."

For a moment nobody stirred. Then the people slowly left the square, and the British officers marched the soldiers back to their posts.

Early the next morning, Samuel Adams and Dr. Joseph Warren went to Beacon Hill to talk with John Hancock.

"Yes, it was awful work!" Dr. Warren exclaimed. "Four Bostonians were killed and a fifth, Patrick Carr, will die of his wounds."

"It was a massacre," said Samuel Adams. "At least, I shall describe it as a massacre in the letter I mean to write to the King. I've sent a message to Thomas Hutchinson, telling him that the soldiers must be removed from Boston or more deaths may occur."

John Hancock frowned. "Captain Preston, Hugh Montgomery, and the seven main guardsmen were arrested and thrown into prison before sunrise. They will be tried for murder. It is important that they have a fair trial — important for our sake, as well as theirs. But where is the lawyer who will defend them?"

At eleven o'clock that morning a thousand people were in Faneuil Hall, waiting for Thomas Hutchinson's answer to Samuel Adams's message. When no answer was received, a committee of fifteen citizens, headed by Samuel Adams and John Hancock, went to the Town House, where the lieutenant governor was meeting with other royal officials.

"I cannot do as you ask, gentlemen," Thomas Hutchinson said to the committee. "I am not in control of the King's troops."

John Hancock spoke. "Sir, we warn you that the people are very excited."

The lieutenant governor knew that John Hancock was a man of sense and judgment. He said slowly, "Perhaps I can have one regiment sent to Castle Island."

The committee went back to Faneuil Hall

and Samuel Adams mounted the platform to
report what Hutchinson had said.

"But, my friends," Samuel Adams cried, "I
think it must be both regiments or none!"

"Yes, yes," the people chanted. *"Both regiments or none!"*

It was nearly dark and snow was falling as
the committee went again to the Town House.
The King's men, in powdered wigs and scarlet cloaks, sat in an upper room. They looked
grave.

"Mr. Hutchinson, it is our view that if you can remove one regiment of soldiers, you can remove two," John Hancock said.

Samuel Adams shook his finger at the lieutenant governor. "Sir, the people of Massachusetts are growing impatient. They want justice and they will not wait forever!"

The officials whispered together; then Hutchinson rose. "Gentlemen," he said, "you may tell the people that both regiments will be removed."

JOHN HANCOCK: FRIEND OF FREEDOM

Three weeks later, on a brisk spring day, the redcoats marched down the Long Wharf to the small boats that plied between Boston and Castle Island. Bostonians were glad to see them go. *"Lobsters!"* they cried. *"Hup-hup! Who buys lobsters?"*

And the soldiers weren't sorry to be going. "It is an uncivilized town," said one British captain. "Full of savages!"

In the autumn, Captain Preston, Montgomery, and the seven guardsmen were tried for murder. Their lawyers were Josiah Quincy and John Adams.

Many friends of John Adams thought it strange that he should help these Britishers. He was a member of the Sons of Liberty and had often opposed measures of the King and Parliament. But he was a good lawyer and a very honest man. He did not believe that the Britishers had committed murder. Captain Preston had sworn that he was not the person who shouted *"Fire!"* on the night of the massacre, and John Adams felt that Captain Preston was telling the truth.

"The soldiers feared for their lives," the Captain said. "They were only defending themselves from the mob."

And Patrick Carr, the fifth Bostonian to die, had said on his deathbed, "I believe that if the soldiers had not fired, they would all have been killed."

John Adams thought, as did Hancock, that it was extremely important for every man to have a fair trial. John Hancock had once said, "How can we demand justice for ourselves if we deny it to others?" John Adams agreed with him.

Captain Preston was tried first, in October. He was found not guilty. In November, a jury found six of the guardsmen not guilty, and discharged them, but Hugh Montgomery and one guardsman, Matthew Killroy, were found guilty of manslaughter. The two men were branded on their thumbs with a white-hot iron and then set free.

The Liberty Tree.

CHAPTER 10

A Mysterious Tea Party

LIBERTY TREE After the removal of the British troops, Boston seemed quite peaceful. For a time, the King was more considerate of his American colonists. The Townshend Acts were repealed, except for the tax on tea. The King held on stubbornly to the tea tax. He saw it as a proof that he had the right to tax his subjects if he wanted to.

"But we do not have to drink tea!" the Americans said. "Tea drinking is only a habit. We will cure ourselves of the habit!"

John Hancock thought that this period of peace probably would not last, so he made the most of it. He worked hard at his business, and even harder for the good of his fellow citizens. He bought a fire engine for Boston. He gave a library of books to Harvard College. He gave bells, pews, and silver communion services to Massachusetts churches, in memory of his father and of his Uncle Thomas.

The Boston streets were dark at night. He bought lamps to light them. He drew plans for a public park on Beacon Hill, which would have flower beds, shady paths, and a fenced-in playground for children. He gave summer picnics on Boston Common and feasted the poor people of the town with barbecued beef and lamb, cakes and pies, beer and cider.

He was very busy in colonial politics. Those Americans who felt that the English government was not fair to them now called themselves patriots or Whigs. Those who supported the King and the royal officials were known as loyalists or Tories. For years, John Hancock had been a Whig member of the Boston Council and the Massachusetts

Assembly. He had become a leader of the Whig Party.

Though most people admired him, there were a few who thought that he was vain and conceited. They made fun of his colorful clothes and said he was "a dressed-up fop," a "Jim-dandy."

"Don't bother about such folks, John! They're just envious," Aunt Lydia told him.

He had been in love once — with pretty Miss Sally Jackson of Boston. They were engaged — until Miss Sally changed her mind and married somebody else.

"Oh, that foolish, *foolish* girl!" Aunt Lydia had said. "How she will regret it! And how cruel of her to break dear John's heart!"

But his heart wasn't broken, nor even cracked. There were lots of pretty girls around and he rather liked being a bachelor. When a Boston Corps of Cadets was formed, he joined it, and he soon was elected its colonel. He liked his military title: "Colonel Hancock!" He bought handsome gold-braided uniforms not only for himself, but for the corps, and he hired a squad of fifers for their drills.

In 1773 Parliament passed the Tea Act. American colonists were displeased, and the patriots of Boston were "ready to boil over" again.

The British East India Company was in danger of going into bankruptcy. Its tea trade with the American colonies had fallen off because the colonists were buying cheaper tea smuggled in from Holland. The Tea Act helped the Company by allowing it to ship tea to American ports without paying the usual heavy tax in England. But the colonists would have to pay a small tax of threepence a pound. Although the colonists would be getting the tea at a low price, they thought the act was a trick to make them forget they were paying a tax on the tea.

Sir Francis Bernard had gone back to England to stay. Thomas Hutchinson was now the royal governor of Massachusetts. Governor Hutchinson announced that the British East India Company was sending to America half a million pounds of tea. The tea ships would land at New York, Philadelphia, Boston, and Charleston, South Carolina.

"This is the last, worst, and most destructive of the King's harsh measures," said the Boston patriots. "We must resist it!"

Three tea ships — the *Dartmouth,* the *Eleanor,* and the *Beaver* — were on the sea, bound for Boston. Weeks before they arrived, the Boston mob was out, threatening Governor Hutchinson's Tory agents and breaking windowpanes in the shops where the tea was to be sold. Every night the political clubs argued in the taprooms of the Green Dragon Tavern and the Salutation. Often in the daytime, John Hancock, Sam Adams, and Dr. Joseph Warren made fiery speeches about the tea tax under the spreading boughs of the Liberty Tree.

The *Dartmouth,* containing one hundred and fourteen chests of tea, sailed into Boston Harbor on November 27. A committee of patriots told her owner, Francis Rotch, that the ship was not to be unloaded. "Have your captain moor the *Dartmouth* at Griffin's Wharf," said the committee.

Mr. Rotch himself was a Bostonian. He said, "I would remind you that if my cargo isn't unloaded within twenty days, the customs officials will seize the ship."

"Yes," the patriots said. "Within twenty days, something may happen."

"What?" Mr. Rotch asked. "What are you thinking of?"

The patriots answered mysteriously, "Something. We'll see."

The next morning there was a public meeting in Faneuil Hall. Samuel Adams presided. "Let us vote to send the *Dartmouth* back to England!" he suggested. But the crowd was so big that a vote could not be taken. "Then let us meet this afternoon in Old South Meeting House, where we shall have more space," he said.

The afternoon meeting was twice as big. The people voted to send the *Dartmouth* back as soon as possible — and without paying a penny of the tax on the tea.

"Meanwhile," said Samuel Adams, "a watch will be kept to see that the ship is not unloaded. Who will volunteer as a watchman?"

Dozens of hands were raised. A young doctor named Thomas Young was seated in the front row. He shouted, "Mr. Adams, I'm not for sending the tea back to England. I'm for throwing it into the harbor!"

John Hancock had gone to the meeting with Paul Revere. He said, "Paul, you and I know that the tax shouldn't be paid. And that it won't be. But how can we send the *Dartmouth* back? Governor Hutchinson has issued an order to the harbor officials that no ship can sail from here unless its captain has papers to show that all cargo has been unloaded."

Paul Revere was now a courier for the Sons of Liberty, delivering messages from town to town in Massachusetts. Strong and athletic, he was a fine horseman. Smiling at his friend John Hancock, he said, "Couldn't we unload the tea ourselves?"

"Ah!" said John Hancock. "That's an idea. Perhaps we could."

"Some of the boys at the Salutation think so." Paul Revere clapped on his cap and looked down at his spurred boots. "I must be off, John. Five of us couriers are riding along the coast. We want to make certain that no tea ships are docked anywhere else in the colony."

On December 2, the *Eleanor* entered Boston Harbor. The *Beaver* came a few days later. Each brought one hundred and fourteen chests of tea. The captains moored the ships at Griffin's Wharf beside the *Dartmouth*. The captains were puzzled. The patriots would not let them unload. Governor Hutchinson was saying that they could not leave the port without unloading.

"What are we to do?" wondered the captains.

On December 16, seven thousand people crowded into Old South Meeting House. It was a cold, rainy afternoon. Samuel Adams, John Hancock, and Josiah Quincy had seats on the platform, behind the pulpit. Today they were waiting for Francis Rotch, who had gone to talk with Governor Hutchinson. Once more Mr. Rotch was asking the governor for the papers that would permit the *Dartmouth* to sail back to England.

John Hancock looked at the waiting people. They were yawning, stretching, dozing. Little children were rubbing their eyes. Babies slept in their mothers' laps. The air was damp and steamy.

The hours went by. The church darkened and candles were lighted. At last, at six o'clock, Francis Rotch came. He walked up the aisle to the pulpit. He looked tired. And, tired as they were, the people strained to hear what he would tell them.

Mr. Rotch said, "I didn't get the papers. The governor is firm. The *Dartmouth* must stay where she is till the tax is paid."

There was silence in the church. Then Samuel Adams got up from his chair and exclaimed, "This meeting can do nothing more to save the country!"

Samuel Adams spoke calmly. But as if his words were a signal, someone in the gallery shouted, "To Griffin's Wharf. Boston Harbor a teapot tonight!" Quickly a chorus of voices echoed, *"To Griffin's Wharf! Boston Harbor a teapot!"*

John Hancock rose to his feet, straight and tall, and the audience stared at him. "Mr. Hancock, what do *you* say?"

He said, *"Let every man do what's right in his own eyes!"*

Less than an hour later, men dressed like Mohawk Indians were running down Griffin's Wharf. There were a hundred and fifty of them. Their faces were smeared with lampblack or burnt cork. They carried axes, tomahawks, and knives. They leaped aboard the three tea ships, hoisted the tea chests from the holds, broke open the chests, and spilled the tea into the harbor. Axes rang on metal, wood snapped and split, the men toiled and sweated. Tons of tea slid over the rails, floated like seaweed, and stained the water brown.

126

On the wharf, hundreds of people watched in silence.

By nine o'clock, all the chests had been emptied. The Mohawks jumped from the ships' decks and strode up the wharf. The watchers followed. From somewhere, a drummer and two fiddlers had come. They struck up a rollicking tune.

"A very interesting tea party, eh?" Paul Revere said to John Hancock as the two friends washed the black from their faces at the Salutation Tavern.

John Hancock laughed. "I enjoyed it. Sit down and drink a mug of ale with me, Paul. Yes, this has been quite an evening." He paused, then said, "And I think the King will punish us for it."

CHAPTER 11

The Shadow
of War

LIBERTY TREE

May 17, 1774, was another day of rain and chill wind in Boston.

John Hancock and his Corps of Cadets were on the Long Wharf that morning. Near them were the Boston militiamen, drawn up in ranks. A short distance away, Thomas Hutchinson stood with a group of royal officials and Tory gentlemen. British battleships lay at anchor in the harbor, and the wheeling gulls seemed to cry mournfully.

King George had wasted no time in punishing the Boston patriots for their Tea Party. He said that the town owed the East India Company for three hundred and forty-two

129

chests of tea. Parliament had passed a bill which would close the port of Boston until the debt was paid. The King had made General Thomas Gage the royal governor of Massachusetts, to replace Thomas Hutchinson, and to rule the colony by military law.

This was the day when General Gage would bring a large army of British troops to the town — many more "lobsters" than had been there before. John Hancock could see people massed on the waterfront. He knew that they would never pay for those tons of tea!

"They are frightened," he said to himself. "The closing of the port will mean that hundreds of men will be out of work and their families hungry. I must open my purse to them."

Since the passage of the Port Bill, Paul Revere had saddled his horse and ridden out to tell the neighboring towns that after June 1, Boston would be cut off from the world.

"No vessels of any sort may sail into the harbor or out of it," Paul Revere told them.

Samuel Adams had written letters north, south, and west, urging the colonists to form Committees of Correspondence.

"Soon our citizens will be like prisoners in a military camp," Samuel Adams wrote. "But we must keep in touch with our sister colonies! We must report to you — and get bulletins from you. Our reports and bulletins must fly back and forth secretly. We must *communicate*."

John Hancock had helped with the forming of Committees of Correspondence in New England. Patriots there, and in most of the southern colonies, were sorry for the people of Boston. They said, "If the King can do this to you, he could be just as cruel to us. The King is becoming a tyrant!" They sent food and money to Boston, gifts which the leaders stored in the Hancock warehouses.

John Hancock thought about all this as he stood with his cadets in the pouring rain. He saw General Gage and his staff officers disembarking from the battleships and getting into the small boats that would carry them ashore. As General Gage stepped onto the Long Wharf, British guns roared a salute. Bugles blew and drums pounded as Hutchinson and Gage shook hands, then walked side by side toward the Town House. There Tory ladies had prepared a banquet to honor the new governor.

"Mr. Hutchinson," General Gage said as they sat at the banquet table, "I observe that Mr. John Hancock is the colonel of a cadet corps. The King would not like that. The King thinks that Hancock is a dangerous man."

"He is a very popular man," said Mr. Hutchinson. "He has great influence with the people."

"It will be well for the cadets to find another colonel," said General Gage.

During the next few weeks the British soldiers filled the town to overflowing. Finally there would be ten thousand of them. General Gage said that from now on Salem, and not Boston, would be the capital of Massachusetts Colony: "And there will be no more sessions of your colonial legislature, unless I think a session is necessary."

One day he called John Hancock to his headquarters. "Your dismissal from the Cadet Corps, sir," he said, handing him a paper.

John Hancock was not surprised. He accepted the paper and folded it into his pocket, knowing that he could do nothing else. But the cadets, when they heard of his dismissal, were furious.

"Then we'll all resign!" they said.

That evening their sergeant went to General Gage, clicked his heels, and said, "Sir, we have been a volunteer corps, not regular militiamen. We will not have any other colonel than John Hancock. You have dismissed him — and we are dissolving the corps. It no longer exists!"

John Hancock did not worry about the dissolved Cadet Corps. Other worries were uppermost in his mind. Parliament had passed a series of laws known in England as the Coercive Acts — and in the colonies as the

Intolerable Acts. They robbed the colonists of more of their rights. John Hancock began to feel, as Samuel Adams did, that war with England could not be avoided.

In the summer, the Massachusetts legislators met in Salem. They met without General Gage's consent or knowledge. The legislatures of New York and Rhode Island had suggested that a Continental Congress be held somewhere, with each colony sending delegates. The Massachusetts legislators wanted to discuss this suggestion.

As they were talking, somebody knocked on the door.

"Who is it?" asked Samuel Adams.

John Hancock glanced from the window. "It's Gage's secretary! Gage must have learned about our meeting!"

Adams sped to the door and locked it.

The secretary knocked and knocked, then went away, red-faced with anger.

The legislators voted to have the Continental Congress meet in Philadelphia in September. They elected five men to be the

Massachusetts delegates. These five were Samuel and John Adams, Thomas Cushing, James Bowdoin, and Robert Treat Paine.

John Hancock had not wanted to be a delegate. The trip would be long and the men might be gone for months. And Hancock had fallen in love again! — this time with charming Miss Dorothy Quincy. If he stayed in Boston, he would be near her. "Miss Dolly" hadn't said that she would marry him.

"But she hasn't said she *wouldn't*," he told Aunt Lydia. "I am hopeful."

As summer came on, the patriots of Massachusetts seemed to have many secrets. They bought guns, bayonets, bombshells, spades, pickaxes, and canvas for tents, all the things an army might use. They hid their supplies in country churchyards and deserted barns and stables. The militiamen drilled on dozens of village greens. Many companies of volunteer soldiers were recruited. Such soldiers were nicknamed "minutemen," because they could be called up at a minute's notice to join the militia.

It was a hot summer — a terrible summer for General Gage! The Americans were so annoying! Why, he could do nothing with them! He tried to organize a governor's council, but couldn't get anyone to serve on it. He couldn't get judges or sheriffs to hold court in the colony. How on earth could he enforce the laws if there were no courts!

And though many Bostonians had no jobs now, they wouldn't work for him! He wanted to build barracks for his troops. He said he would hire Boston carpenters and masons at high wages. They said, "No thanks. We'd rather be idle."

The Sons of Liberty were smuggling guns and ammunition from the British camps. Yes, and cannons! General Gage knew it, but he seemed unable to put a stop to it. One dark night four great cannons vanished from Boston Common. General Gage's Tory spies told him that whole families of Bostonians, fathers and mothers and children, were making bullets and cartridges in their kitchens by candlelight.

"How defiant they are!" said the General, fuming.

And he was having the oddest accidents nowadays! Barges bringing bricks for his barracks somehow sank in shallow water. Wagons loaded with lumber were upset or bogged down on muddy roads. Straw for his troopers' beds caught fire and burned to ashes.

"Surely the rebels are at the bottom of this," he said, "for I cannot think we are bewitched!"

"Poor Gage, I am almost sorry for him," John Hancock said to Samuel Adams. "But I'm proud that our people are showing so much spirit."

The five Massachusetts delegates to the Continental Congress were to start for Philadelphia on August 10. They gathered that morning in Thomas Cushing's house. Their wives and friends and many members of the Sons of Liberty were there to bid them goodby. They would travel in style, for John Hancock had lent them a coach for the journey. The coach was new, painted black with red-and-yellow-striped wheels.

After a lunch of biscuits, fruit, and punch, John Hancock made a speech wishing the delegates Godspeed. Toasts were drunk to everyone's health and to the glorious cause of freedom.

Samuel Adams wrote John Hancock a letter from Philadelphia. He said that the Congress had addressed messages to the King, to the people of the American colonies, and to the people of Quebec and Great Britain.

These messages were very mild in tone. They contained a list of the rights which, the delegates thought, had been taken from the colonists since 1763. The delegates said that the colonists wanted peace, but they also wanted relief from oppression. The colonists were not represented in Parliament and could not be so represented. Therefore, they should not be taxed by Parliament. The message to the people of England asked for their understanding and sympathy. Nothing was said about rebellion or a possible war between the colonies and the mother country.

Samuel Adams also said that the delegates had voted to form an Association of the colonies, and had agreed not to import any goods from Great Britain or Ireland, nor any East India tea, nor any of certain products from the West Indies.

John Hancock did not believe that the King would heed what the Continental Congress did. "The King has never heeded us; he isn't likely to change now," he said to Paul Revere and Dr. Warren. "This Association may make him realize that we can unite. I think it is important."

Hancock answered Adams's letter. He had bad news: "Parties of British soldiers have raided the buildings at Charlestown and Cambridge in which the Sons of Liberty have kept our stores. Hundreds of barrels of our gunpowder were taken. Gage has stationed guards all around Boston. Day and night the sentries prowl our streets. Spies are everywhere and trouble is in the wind."

General Gage had done away with the Massachusetts legislature. He said it could never meet again — in Salem, or anywhere else.

"There *is* no Massachusetts legislature," General Gage said. "It is abolished — dead, a thing of the past. From now on the King and Parliament will make the laws for this colony. And I will make you people toe the line!"

But just the same, two hundred and sixty determined patriots went to Salem early in October. There they organized a Provincial

Congress and elected John Hancock as its president.

"The King and Parliament may make laws for us," said John Hancock. "But as for 'toeing' Gage's line — we shall see about that!"

CHAPTER 12

Midnight Alarm

LIBERTY TREE As John Hancock had said, the King's feeling about his American colonists had not changed. George III had never been a patient man. He was not patient now.

"The colonists must be taught a lesson they'll not forget — even if it means having a war," he told his ministers in London.

But General Gage really did not want to begin a war. He said to himself, "I'll get possession of the Americans' military supplies and arrest some of their most powerful leaders. And that, I think, will tame them!"

Every year since the Boston Massacre, a memorial service had been held on March 5 in the Old South Meeting House. In 1775, March 5 was a Sunday, so the event was to

143

take place on Monday. Dr. Warren was to preach the sermon and John Hancock would make a short speech. As president of the Provincial Congress and chairman of a newly formed Committee of Safety, Hancock had more power than any other Boston patriot.

Gage sent three hundred of his soldiers to the church on March 6. The soldiers were grinning, for they had a plan. One of their officers had an egg in his pocket. The plan was that the officer should throw the egg into Dr. Warren's face. Then the redcoats would pounce upon Warren, Hancock, and Samuel Adams and haul them off to jail as traitors.

But the plan failed. The church was so packed that the egg was smashed in the officer's pocket. The soldiers had to listen to Dr. Warren and John Hancock denouncing the King and Parliament. Though the Britishers hooted and yelled, and afterward rioted in the streets, they were disappointed.

The Provincial Congress had no fixed meeting place. It moved from town to town. On April 15, 1775, it met in Concord. That evening John Hancock with his secretary, John Lowell, and Samuel Adams drove in his grand coach to the parsonage of the Reverend Mr. Jonas Clark. The parsonage was a quarter-mile northeast of the village of Lexington. Mr. Clark's wife was a cousin of John Hancock's. Aunt Lydia and Miss Dolly Quincy would also be there. John Hancock and Miss Dolly were now engaged to be married and he eagerly looked forward to seeing her.

"I think we'd best stay out of Boston for a while, Sam," he said to Samuel Adams. "You know that some of the Tories are threatening to murder us? I've told my aunt that she and Dolly must not go back there.

"And the Tories say they will burn down my Beacon Hill house," he added. "Last week they burned the fences around my garden, you know."

"And much of your business property is in ruins," Samuel Adams said. "Your work for liberty is costing you a great amount of money, Hancock!"

"That doesn't matter," Hancock said. "Let

145

the King, the Tories, and Gage make me a
beggar — if the public benefit requires it."
He added, "I believe that war will soon be
upon us."

But the next day, at the Clarks', was very
quiet. It was Sunday. John Hancock attended Mr. Clark's church and prayed with
the congregation for justice and peace in the
land. He was happy to be with Aunt Lydia
and Dolly Quincy again. Dolly was slender,
brown-haired and bright-eyed. She was something of a tease, and her manner was gay and
laughing. Aunt Lydia beamed at her nephew
and told everybody how famous he was.

"Dear John!" she said. "Always such a
good boy!"

Smiling, he said, "Scarcely a boy now,
Aunt Lydia. I'm thirty-eight."

In the afternoon Paul Revere, on his big
gray horse, cantered into the parsonage lane.

"I slipped past Gage's guards," he said to
John Hancock. "The small boats belonging
to those British ships in the harbor were all
repaired yesterday. I thought you ought to

know it. The boats must be going somewhere."

"Where?" Hancock asked.

Paul Revere shrugged. "No telling. I'll bet that Gage has some scheme up his sleeve. You and Adams are delegates to the Second Continental Congress in May. I advise you to go on to Philadelphia from here."

John Hancock nodded. "Good advice. You and Warren must be on the watch, Paul. Let me know if there are further signs of trouble."

Monday was another quiet day, but on Tuesday a few British soldiers were seen on the roads between Boston and Lexington. In the evening, eight Lexington militiamen came to the Clark house. The sergeant, William Munroe, said that their captain had ordered them to patrol there tonight.

"We've heard tales of spies roundabout, Mr. Hancock," said the sergeant.

The Clark family and their guests went to bed early, but Hancock could not sleep. It was a beautiful moonlit night. He tossed on

his pillows. At midnight, he got up, put on his dressing gown, and stood at a window. He could see Sergeant Munroe and the sentries pacing in the yard.

Suddenly there was the clatter of hoofs. A lone horseman galloped through the gate.

Sergeant Munroe ran forward. "Halt! No noise, please! Mr. Clark's folks are all asleep —"

The horseman interrupted. "Noise! You'll have noise enough before long! The British are marching!"

John Hancock knew that voice. He called, "Revere! Come in!"

Paul Revere went into the house and breathlessly told his story. The British were on their way to Concord to get the guns and ammunition which the colonists had stored there. They would march through Lexington — a thousand or more of them! It was to have been a secret, but the secret had leaked out. Dr. Warren had sent two Sons of Liberty couriers, Paul Revere and William Dawes, to spread the alarm. The couriers had taken

different routes. Revere had rowed across the Charles River in a borrowed skiff, then galloped thirteen miles on a borrowed horse.

Now all the people in the house were awake, clustering about Paul Revere.

"The militia and minutemen will muster on Lexington green," John Hancock said. "I'll join them! Where's my sword? Fetch my gun, somebody!"

"No, no, John!" Aunt Lydia shrieked.

"My place is on the firing line, ma'am!"

"Indeed, it is not," said Samuel Adams. "If you show yourself, you'll be killed — or captured. You and I have something else far more important to do for the cause of liberty. We must make our way toward Philadelphia. I know that you're not a coward, Hancock. I also know that you're worth more to America alive than dead!"

A moment later William Dawes reached the parsonage. He had ridden sixteen miles and had aroused many towns and villages. He said that patriots were hurrying toward Concord from all corners of Massachusetts.

At one o'clock, Paul Revere and William Dawes remounted and set out for Concord. Mrs. Clark and her children bundled themselves into a wagon, and a servant drove them to her father's farm, which was nearby. Aunt Lydia and Dolly Quincy decided to remain in the parsonage with Mr. Clark. Dolly vowed that she wasn't afraid: "Rascals though they are, the British would not harm women!"

Aunt Lydia wailed that she simply could not travel. "I am trembling like a leaf!" she said.

John Hancock still thought it was his duty to join the militiamen. As he argued with Samuel Adams about it, Paul Revere reappeared in the parsonage yard. Revere was weary and groaning. At the outskirts of Lexington, he and William Dawes had been overtaken by Samuel Prescott, a young doctor whose home was in Concord.

"Prescott wanted to ride with us," said Paul Revere. "We were pushing on when we saw British soldiers looming up ahead of us. They were blocking the road. Dawes jerked his reins and dodged them, but Prescott and I were caught. The Britishers herded us into a fenced field where they had other prisoners. Prescott put spurs to his horse. The horse jumped the fence and he got away. I had no chance to escape. After an hour, a redcoat major said that he wanted my horse — it was of some use to him. But I was not. He let me go and I walked back here."

By this time the secretary, Mr. Lowell, had harnessed a horse to Mr. Clark's phaeton and brought the light carriage to the door. Adams had persuaded Hancock to drive to the town of Woburn.

"Come with us, Paul," John Hancock said. "We may need a courier."

The four men got into the phaeton, but they had not gone far when Mr. Lowell cried, "Oh, Mr. Hancock, your trunk! I left it in the Lexington tavern."

"You'll have to go back for it," John Hancock said. "The Provincial Congress papers are in that trunk. But it's too heavy for you to carry alone."

"I'll help Mr. Lowell," Paul Revere said. "Don't wait for us, Hancock. Drive on as fast as you can. We'll fetch the trunk to Woburn tonight."

Hancock and Adams drove on. It was five o'clock now, a warm and sparkling spring morning — April 19, 1775.

John Hancock heard, faintly and far off, the sound of guns. He thought of what might be happening at Lexington. Was this the beginning of a war?

"If so, the colonists must win it," he said to himself. *"We must!"*

CHAPTER 13

War and
a Noble Document

John Hancock and Samuel Adams did not stay long in Woburn. They went on toward Philadelphia, where the Second Continental Congress was to meet on May 10. As they traveled, they learned that the colonial militiamen had clashed with the British regulars at Lexington and again at Concord. At first, the Americans had been overwhelmed, but soon patriot soldiers from towns roundabout had hastened to the scene. The British did not find the military stores they were hunting for in Concord. And American sharpshooters had chased them all the way back to Boston. The day had been, in fact, a triumph for the Massachusetts militia and minutemen.

Now the patriots knew that they were really at war with England. They must fight, not only for their rights, but for their very lives. They knew that the Tories in the colonies would be on the King's side and that many other people would have no part in this war on either side.

The Tories boasted of the King's army of thousands of well-trained soldiers, and the English navy, which was the biggest in the world. "The King is rich. He can provide his troops with everything they need. The colonial legislatures are poor. Their soldiers are ragtag, bobtail villagers and raw recruits. And the colonies have no navy at all."

The patriots replied, "But we have a just cause! Our ideals will make us strong."

The delegates to the Continental Congress were cheered and applauded as they gathered in Philadelphia. The loudest cheering was for John Hancock, the most widely known of them all. In a letter to Dolly Quincy, he said,

"I have been saluted everywhere with cannon and with music. At New York, I was hailed by vast crowds, who took the horses from my phaeton and pulled it themselves through the city. Entering Philadelphia, I was trailed by scores of marchers, decorated carriages, and prancing horsemen."

157

When the Congress opened, John Hancock was elected as its president.

He was pleased to be in a position of such honor, but knew that he faced tremendous tasks. The Congress would be the governing body of the colonies during this troubled time. It must enlist and drill a proper army. The soldiers would have to be fed, clothed, and paid wages, so that their families at home would not starve. And, somehow, a navy must be built, for England would strike by sea as well as by land.

The Congress appointed George Washington of Virginia to head the American forces. On July 3, at Cambridge, Massachusetts, George Washington took command of about twenty thousand men and officers. But already one historic battle had been fought. On the night of June 16, American soldiers had camped upon Breed's Hill, which overlooked Charlestown and Boston. They had intended to fortify nearby Bunker Hill, but had passed it in the dark. On June 17, the Americans had been attacked by Gage's troops and driven to retreat. The action would be known as the Battle of Bunker Hill. Though the British were victorious that day, their losses were far greater than those of the Americans. The siege of Boston would continue for many more months.

John Hancock had little rest. All summer he worked hard. The delegates often disagreed among themselves. If Hancock had not been a good leader, the Congress might not have accomplished much. He could get along with people. They trusted him, and he could smooth their ruffled tempers. Even so, he had some hot arguments and made some political enemies.

After the fighting at Lexington and Concord, many patriots had slipped away from Boston to live in other towns. Aunt Lydia Hancock and Dolly Quincy had been visiting at the home of their friends Mr. and Mrs. Thaddeus Burr, in Fairfield, Connecticut. John Hancock had sent handsome presents to Dolly and letters begging her to set a date for their wedding.

In the last week of August, he went to Fairfield and they were married. He wore a suit of crimson velvet at the wedding, and Dolly looked lovely in her white gown and veil.

Aunt Lydia wept and smiled and called them her dear, dear children.

"Oh, how this marriage delights me!" said Aunt Lydia.

A furnished apartment in Philadelphia was the first home of the bride and bridegroom. It was small and plain.

"But never mind, Dolly," said Hancock. "Some day we'll go back to the Beacon Hill house — that is, if it's still there!"

In March of the next year, 1776, George Washington's troops advanced toward Boston, and the British boarded their transport ships and sailed from the harbor to seek a new base.

The Bostonians who went back to their town were shocked by its appearance. The British had chopped down hundreds of trees. Sheds, barns, cottages had been torn down and the lumber burned as firewood during the cold winter months. Shops, churches, and many large houses had been wrecked. But John and Dolly found that the Hancock house was not badly damaged. British officers had been living in it. The stables and coach house had been used as a hospital.

Hancock wrote to Aunt Lydia that he would have the house repainted and cleaned up for her. He said that she and Dolly would be safe there, cared for by Cato, Seth, and the other old servants. But Aunt Lydia was never to see the house again. In April, she died suddenly in Fairfield.

John Hancock was very sad. He had been devoted to her always. "I shall miss her kindness and affection," he said. "I loved her."

At the war's beginning, the American patriots had thought of themselves as British subjects whom the King slighted and mistreated. Only a few of them had ever thought that the colonies should separate entirely from England. But as the months passed, they were more and more convinced that they must be a new nation, with a government all their own.

"There is too much difference between what the King believes and what we believe," they said. "Our quarrel with him has gone on for too long. We cannot settle our differences now. We do not want George III to rule us. We do not want any king, not even a good one."

On June 7, 1776, Richard Henry Lee of

Virginia read some resolutions to his fellow members of the Continental Congress. The resolutions said that "these United Colonies are, and of right ought to be, free and independent states; that they are absolved from all allegiance to the British Crown, and that all political connection between them and the State of Great Britain is, and ought to be, totally dissolved."

John Hancock, as president of the Congress, appointed a committee of five men — Thomas Jefferson, Benjamin Franklin, John Adams, Roger Sherman, and Robert R. Livingston — to draft a declaration of independence. John Hancock knew that this was a daring step for the colonies to take, a history-making step. But he heartily favored it. His country, he felt, must be free.

Thomas Jefferson wrote the Declaration, with Benjamin Franklin and John Adams adding to it here and there. In it Thomas Jefferson told why it was necessary for the Americans to make such a declaration. He recounted all the tyrannical acts of the King.

He said that often the colonists had appealed most humbly to the King, and to the English people, for justice. But "our repeated petitions," he said, "have been answered only by repeated injury." He quoted from Lee's resolutions. In conclusion, he said that for the support of this declaration, the members of the Congress pledged to each other their lives, their fortunes, and their sacred honor.

On July 2, the Congress voted for Lee's resolutions. On the afternoon of July 4, the Declaration of Independence was presented to the Congress and was accepted. This first draft was written on a sheet of plain paper.

"But it must be written on parchment," said Hancock, "and copies of it must be sent to all the colonial legislatures and to General Washington. Our armies must know of this Declaration, wherever they are. The whole world must know!"

The copies which he ordered were printed that night. The next morning he sent them off by messenger, thinking as he did so that he was taking upon himself the whole responsibility for the colonies' rebellion and branding himself as a traitor to the King.

On August 2, the official copy of the Declaration, penned large on a sheet of parchment, was put before the Congress for the signatures of the members.

John Hancock was the first man to sign the great document.

Clearly and beautifully he wrote his name, as he had been taught to write it so long ago in the Boston Latin School.

"There!" he said, smiling and looking up into the earnest faces that surrounded him. "There! John Bull can read my name without spectacles. That is my defiance!"

CHAPTER 14

A Statesman's Tasks

LIBERTY TREE Americans celebrated the sign-
ing of the Declaration of Independence with
chiming church bells and gay parades in
every town and village. They seemed to feel
a new pride in their country. How inspiring
it was to be thirteen *states* instead of thirteen
colonies! They repeated to themselves the
noble words Thomas Jefferson had written,
that "all men are created equal." How good
it was to know that all men have certain
rights which cannot be taken from them, that
"among these are life, liberty, and the pursuit
of happiness."

In Boston, lighted candles were set in the
windows of houses and shops, turning night
into day. Children danced in the streets,

singing "Yankee Doodle" and other American songs. In New York City, the celebration was wilder. English flags were stripped from public buildings, and a statue of George III was knocked to the ground and smashed to bits.

Now that the colonies had broken away from England, the French government offered to help them.

"We will lend you troops, guns, ammunition, and the assistance of our navy," France said.

Americans were grateful for France's friendship. They knew that they were not well equipped for war, and this war might be a long one.

As the fighting grew fiercer, some members of the Continental Congress became critical of George Washington. When a battle was lost, they blamed him. They said, "General Washington is too slow. Maybe we should get a commander in chief who will move faster to crush the British under his heel." And some of them said, "Maybe we should make peace with England before we're crushed under the King's heel!"

John Hancock did not listen to these complainers. He had faith in General Washington and never doubted that at last the United States would win the war.

This was not an easy time for John Hancock. There were men in the Congress who were jealous of him and set themselves against any measure that he proposed. His health was not good. He suffered terribly from gout and the headaches which, it seemed, could never be cured. Worst of all, the baby daughter born to him and Dolly in December, 1776, died at the age of nine months. The little girl, named Lydia, had been the darling of her parents, and they mourned for her. Still, Hancock did not despair. He only worked and prayed the more for victory and peace.

He worried about the soldiers. Often they did not have enough to eat. Very few of them had uniforms, and their clothes were patched and ragged. In winter they were cold. Many of them were ill. Many died because they lacked medicines and blankets. The Continental Congress could not always raise the money with which to buy such things. And the promised help from France was slow in coming.

John Hancock said to Dolly, "Not as president of the Congress, but as a private citizen, I must do what I can for our men in the field."

What he did was to give large sums of his own money, to be spent on the needs of the soldiers. He asked other rich men for donations. He said to his wealthy friends, "If you can't — or won't — give money, let me have your old clothes — shirts, shoes, trousers, and coats! My servants will collect them and deliver them to the army camps."

In the autumn of 1777, the British general Lord Howe captured Philadelphia. Just before Howe's regiments marched into the city, the Continental Congress fled, bag and baggage, to Lancaster and then to the town of York, Pennsylvania.

John Hancock believed that Howe did not intend to fight during the winter. He asked Congress to grant him a leave of absence. He had been on duty for two years and five months without a pause.

The request was granted and he started for Boston in a rented carriage. But General Washington had ordered a party of dragoon soldiers, mounted on horses, to guard him.

When he had gone only five miles, the dragoons arrived to trot beside him. Then Dolly came to meet him, riding in one of the Hancock coaches, with footmen on the box and grooms riding behind. As they neared Boston, people ran out of their houses, waving and calling to him, "Hurrah for President Hancock!"

"I'm a lucky man, Dolly," he said. "My friends remember me."

She smiled. "And why not, John? When have you forgotten them? It's said in Boston that no man was ever more beloved by the common folk."

After a short vacation he went back to the Congress, but in 1778 he asked for, and was given, a commission as a major general of the militia. He had always wanted to be a soldier.

"I want the experience of being in a battle," he said.

He was at home when his son, John George Washington Hancock, was born in the spring. Then in the summer he went with American troops who planned to seize the British garrison at Newport, Rhode Island.

For three weeks the Americans camped outside of Newport, waiting for the French fleet to come and bombard the British stronghold from the sea. But storms delayed the French ships. And when the Americans finally attacked, they were blasted by the British cannon and had to retreat.

That was John Hancock's only experience in battle. The marching and the rough life in camp made him sick. His head ached miserably again, and his doctors advised him to retire from the army.

"You are not cut out to be a soldier, sir," the doctors said.

He sighed and nodded. "I suppose that's true."

Now some of the colonies were organizing as states. John Hancock was a member of the convention that drew up a constitution, or body of laws, for the state of Massachusetts in 1780. And when it was time to choose state officials, the people elected him

173

as their first governor. Standing on the State House balcony, while cannon roared and the crowd shouted and clapped, he was proclaimed as "His Excellency John Hancock, Esquire, Governor of the Massachusetts Commonwealth."*

The war was dragging on, and everywhere Americans were weary of the long struggle. Governor Hancock wanted to lift the spirits of his people and give them hope. He encouraged them to have simple entertainments. He arranged for public picnics and band concerts, and opened the theaters in Boston. He encouraged young men to enlist in the militia and saw to it that the Massachusetts regiments were properly trained. He framed laws that would protect the new state.

And at election time the next year, he was re-elected.

* After 1775 the Town House was called the State House.

CHAPTER 15

A Famous Governor

In the summer of 1781, a large British army commanded by Lord Cornwallis was at Yorktown, Virginia. Lord Cornwallis had thought of Yorktown as a good place for an encampment, but George Washington thought of it as a place where the British might be trapped. General Washington marched into Virginia and laid siege to Yorktown. For three weeks he hammered and battered at the British defenses — and on October 19, Cornwallis surrendered his sword, his troops, and his guns.

The battle of Yorktown was the last event in the American Revolution. After six long years of fighting, the war was finally over.

The people of the United States rejoiced. "Now we can look forward to peace, with freedom," they said.

But they found that peace also had its problems. Now they realized how destructive the war had been. Farms were neglected, business and trade at a standstill. The thousands of soldiers who returned to their homes saw that they would have to plow and plant, mend and rebuild.

Political leaders knew that something must be done about laws and government.

"We won the war by working together," the leaders said. "If we don't learn to work together in time of peace, our Union will be worthless. All our toil and sacrifice will have been in vain."

Washington, Franklin, Hancock, and other wise men said, "Let us firmly establish all our thirteen state governments, then form a strong central, or federal, government."

In 1783 John Hancock was elected to his third term as governor of Massachusetts. In

1785 his friends begged him to be a candidate again, but he refused.

"I am not well," he told them. "I cannot continue in the office."

Later that year he was elected to his old position in the Continental Congress. His health seemed better, and he was anxious to visit Philadelphia once more. But on the day that he had expected to leave Boston, he was very sick. He postponed his leave-taking. He heard that the other members of the Congress had voted for him to be their president. A house had been rented for him.

"I must go!" he said.

His doctors shook their heads. "No, no," they warned. "Impossible, Mr. Hancock."

So he stayed in Boston, and managed to keep in touch with what was happening in distant parts of the country. George Washington was saying that the United States must have a set of federal laws, a Constitution. Washington suggested that a convention be held, with delegates from all the states meeting to decide on these laws.

John Hancock liked the idea. "How can I help with it?" he asked himself.

In January, 1787, his nine-year-old son was killed in a skating accident. Though this was the greatest sorrow of John Hancock's life, he bore it bravely and comforted Dolly as best he could. And in April he consented to run for a fourth term as governor. He was elected by a bigger vote than ever before. He had a special reason for wanting to be governor just then.

"I believe that I may be of special service to both my state and the nation," he said.

The Constitutional Convention met in May, 1787, at Philadelphia. For weeks and weeks the delegates studied and debated. It was a very serious matter to draft a set of laws that would be fair to all citizens and all sections.

John Hancock, in Boston, eagerly followed the progress of the convention. He read newspaper accounts of it and received letters from the delegates. In September, when many different views had been stated and compromises made, the convention finished its work.

"A Constitution has been framed," he told Dolly. "But it cannot become the law of the land until the thirteen states have considered it and nine of them have voted to accept, or ratify, it."

"Will this be done by the state legislatures?" asked Dolly.

"No," he answered. "There will be state conventions, to which delegates are elected."

John Hancock carefully read the copy of the Constitution that was sent to him. He approved of it. "We must be a nation united by law or we'll fall to pieces," he said. "I am determined that Massachusetts shall ratify. As governor, I'll have the opportunity to influence our people."

Delaware, Pennsylvania, New Jersey, Georgia, and Connecticut accepted the Constitution. And then Massachusetts did so. Some of the delegates to the state convention had been against it, but because of Governor Hancock, a majority of them were for it.

Hancock felt that this was his special service to Massachusetts and to the nation. "I have never performed a more important one," he said.

Maryland and South Carolina were the seventh and eighth states to ratify, and New Hampshire was the ninth. Soon afterward, the other four states voted for the Constitution. A new federal government was then organized. And in January, 1789, George Washington was unanimously chosen as the first President of the United States.

Many Americans had thought that John Hancock might be the Vice-President. They said that he was almost as famous as George Washington — and no one could be more popular! But the honor went to John Adams. Though Hancock was ill with a fever in 1789, he was re-elected to the governorship of Massachusetts. In 1791, he was again elected. It seemed that as surely as voting time rolled around, the people of the state flocked to the polls to cast their ballots for him.

In 1793, Governor Hancock was elected

to his seventh term of office. He was fifty-six, but looked older. He was stooped and thin and had difficulty in walking. Sometimes he had to be carried out to the coach which took him from Beacon Hill to his duties at the State House. But he insisted on going to work every morning. He said that he might be lame in the legs, but there was nothing wrong with his mind!

At home with Dolly in the evenings, reading or writing, he wore brightly colored dressing gowns, crimson, purple, or bottle green, and a velvet cap with a tassel on it. He

smiled and thought of Uncle Thomas: "You didn't know my uncle, did you, Dolly? He liked to see people looking well. He often said that fine birds deserve fine feathers. Uncle Thomas thought of me as a fine bird. He liked to see me in fine feathers."

His health was failing, and he made his will. His wealth was not what it had been. Huge amounts of his money had gone to charity and still more into the war effort. But there would be enough for Dolly, and something for his mother, who was an old lady now. There would be gifts for his brother, Ebenezer, and for Harvard College, and hospitals and schools.

He died on October 8, 1793. He had said that he wanted his funeral to be small and quiet. "No display, no fuss," he had said. But his friends would not have it so. For a week, houses in Boston were draped with black streamers. All flags in the town and on ships in the harbor flew at half-mast. On the day of the funeral, stores and shops were closed. Church bells rang solemnly every hour.

The funeral procession, several miles long, wound through the hushed streets of the city he had loved, and for which he had done so much. Riding in front were Vice-President Adams and other representatives of the federal government. Next came the carriages of judges and professors, ministers from foreign countries, church officials, generals, and admirals. Behind the carriages marched columns of soldiers, sailors, and marines. Lastly came the plain people of Boston and of Massachusetts. There were more than twenty thousand of them, men, women, and children, the people whom John Hancock had never forgotten, who would remember him always as a great and good American.

old Boston
1775

Charles River

BOSTON COMMON

COMMON ST.

South

End

ORANGE ST.

ESSEX ST.

The

Neck

PURCHASE ST.

1 Beacon Hill
2 Hancock House
3 Liberty Tree
4 Boston Latin School
5 Old South Meeting House
6 Town House

0   1/4   1/2 Mile

SHB

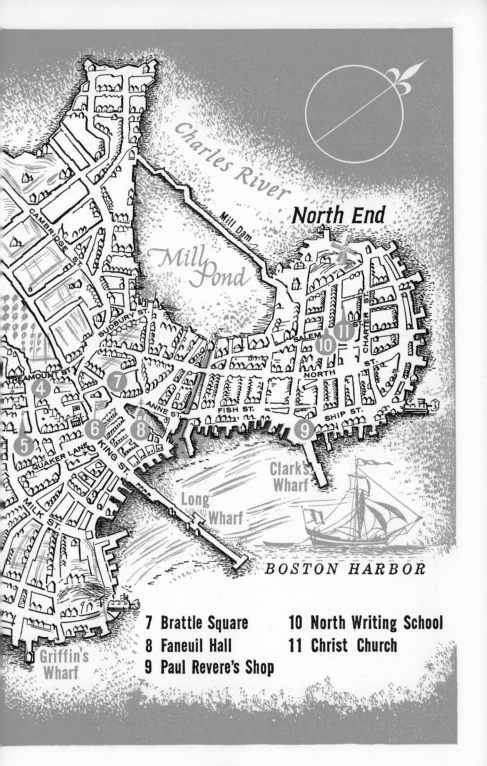

Charles River

North End

Mill Dam

Mill Pond

CAMBRIDGE ST.

SUDBURY ST.

Salem ST.

CHARTER ST.

NORTH ST.

SHIP ST.

TREAMOUNT ST.

ANNE ST.

FISH ST.

KING ST.

QUAKER LANE

MILK ST.

Clark's Wharf

Long Wharf

BOSTON HARBOR

Griffin's Wharf

7 Brattle Square   **10 North Writing School**
8 Faneuil Hall   **11 Christ Church**
9 Paul Revere's Shop

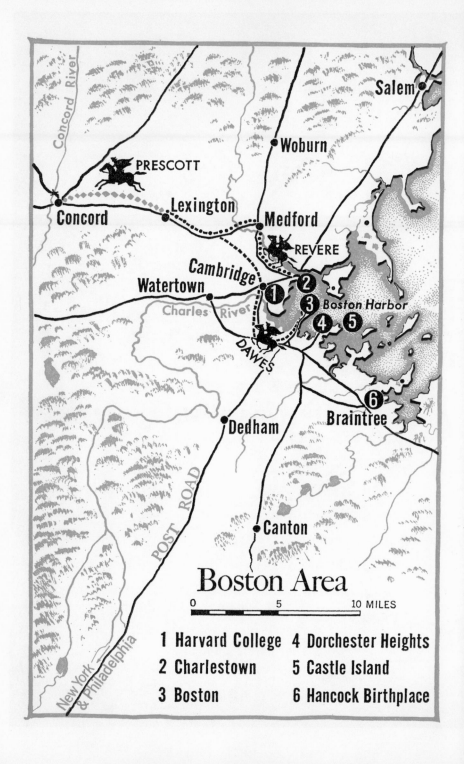

Salem

Concord River

PRESCOTT

Woburn

Concord

Lexington

Medford

REVERE

Cambridge

Watertown

Charles River

Boston Harbor

①

②

③

④

⑤

DAWES

⑥

Braintree

Dedham

Canton

POST ROAD

New York & Philadelphia

Boston Area

0   5   10 MILES

1 Harvard College   4 Dorchester Heights

2 Charlestown   5 Castle Island

3 Boston   6 Hancock Birthplace

Author's Note

When boys and girls of today think of John Hancock, they remember him chiefly as the first man to sign his name to the Declaration of Independence. They have seen copies of this proud and noble document, with John Hancock's big bold signature topping the list of famous names. Perhaps they have visited the National Archives Building in Washington, D.C., where the original Declaration is viewed every year by hundreds of thousands of people from all over the world.

But as Americans we have many other reasons for remembering John Hancock. He was a great patriot. He lived in an exciting and crucial period of history and played an honorable part in all the events of his times. He helped to determine the course of the thirteen colonies as they approached the War of the Revolution. During that struggle, he helped the patriot armies. Afterward, he helped to form and shape the Union of the new states. Indeed, the story of his life is an inspiring chapter in the story of the country he loved and served so well.

In this book, I have given the facts of John Hancock's career. Except for conversations, and minor incidents in the first three chapters, nothing has been invented. Also, I have tried to present him to the reader as the interesting, colorful person his friends knew him to be. These friends were too numerous to be counted and they were of all sorts. It has been said that he had the habit of collecting friends — and of keeping them.

John's health was never strong. Even as a small boy he suffered from the terrible headaches he seemed unable to avoid, and for which no cure ever was found. But his spirit was strong. He was generous and brave.

When John was seven, he was adopted by his Uncle Thomas Hancock and brought to Boston, where he was destined to spend the rest of his life. Thomas Hancock was a very rich merchant, one of the richest men in America. At his death, Thomas Hancock left his fortune to his nephew John. Thomas Hancock had been charitable, but John was even more unselfish. Most of his wealth he used for the good of the community.

As he became a leading citizen of Boston, John Hancock was caught up in the political affairs of the town and of Massachusetts Colony. He became convinced that the colonies must separate from England and establish their own government. He joined the movement for political freedom and was a member of the Sons of Liberty. He was always willing to make the sacrifices necessary for freedom and liberty. It was only fitting that he should have been the first signer of the Declaration proclaiming those splendid ideals which Americans still cherish and guard so carefully.

JEANNETTE C. NOLAN

PIPER BOOKS

ABIGAIL ADAMS: *The President's Lady,* by Regina Z. Kelly
JOHN ALDEN: *Steadfast Pilgrim,* by Cecile Pepin Edwards
ETHAN ALLEN: *Green Mountain Hero,* by Sheldon N. Ripley
HANS CHRISTIAN ANDERSEN: *Fairy Tale Author,* by Shannon Garst
DAN BEARD: *Boy Scout Pioneer,* by Jerry Seibert
DANIEL BOONE: *Wilderness Trailblazer,* by Miriam E. Mason
KIT CARSON: *Mountain Scout,* by Donald E. Worcester
HENRY CLAY: *Statesman and Patriot,* by Regina Z. Kelly
CHRISTOPHER COLUMBUS: *Sailor and Dreamer,* by Bernadine Bailey
AMELIA EARHART: *First Lady of the Air,* by Jerry Seibert
HENRY FORD: *Maker of the Model T,* by Miriam Gilbert
BENJAMIN FRANKLIN: *First Great American,* by John Tottle
JOHN HANCOCK: *Friend of Freedom,* by Jeannette C. Nolan
PATRICK HENRY: *Voice of Liberty,* by William Percival Jones
MATTHEW HENSON: *Arctic Hero,* by Sheldon N. Ripley
SAM HOUSTON: *Friend of the Indians,* by Joseph Olgin
HENRY HUDSON: *Explorer of the North,* by Dorothea J. Snow
THOMAS JEFFERSON: *Champion of the People,* by Joseph Olgin
JOHN PAUL JONES: *Soldier of the Sea,* by Donald E. Worcester
ABRAHAM LINCOLN: *Man of Courage,* by Bernadine Bailey
JAMES MADISON: *Statesman and President,* by Regina Z. Kelly
FERDINAND MAGELLAN: *Noble Captain,* by Katharine Wilkie
HORACE MANN: *Sower of Learning,* by Cecile Pepin Edwards
KING PHILIP: *Loyal Indian,* by Cecile Pepin Edwards
JUAN PONCE DE LEON: *First in the Land,* by Bernadine Bailey
PONTIAC: *Lion in the Forest,* by Wilma Pitchford Hays
JOHN WESLEY POWELL: *Canyon's Conqueror,* by Marian T. Place
PAUL REVERE: *Colonial Craftsman,* by Regina Z. Kelly
SACAJAWEA: *Guide to Lewis and Clark,* by Jerry Seibert
JOHN SMITH: *Man of Adventure,* by Miriam E. Mason
ROBERT LOUIS STEVENSON: *Storyteller and Adventurer,*
    by Katharine Wilkie